FACTORS THAT CONTRIBUTE TO THE
SUCCESS OF SCHOOL PRINCIPALS

EFFECTIVE STRATEGIES FOR SECONDARY SCHOOL PRINCIPALS

FACTORS THAT CONTRIBUTE TO THE SUCCESS OF SCHOOL PRINCIPALS

DR. DINAH A. LARBI

Factors that Contribute to the Success of School Principals
Copyright © 2019 by Dr. Dinah A. Larbi. All rights reserved.

No part of this publication may be reproduced, stored in a retrieval system or transmitted in any way by any means, electronic, mechanical, photocopy, recording or otherwise without the prior permission of the author except as provided by USA copyright law.

The opinions expressed by the author are not necessarily those of URLink Print and Media.

1603 Capitol Ave., Suite 310 Cheyenne, Wyoming USA 82001
1-888-980-6523 | admin@urlinkpublishing.com

URLink Print and Media is committed to excellence in the publishing industry.

Book design copyright © 2019 by URLink Print and Media. All rights reserved.

Published in the United States of America

ISBN 978-1-64367-380-6 (Paperback)
ISBN 978-1-64367-379-0 (Digital)

03.05.19

NOTE TO USERS

This reproduction is the best copy available.

DEDICATION

This book is dedicated to my Lord, my husband
Joe, Kobby, the rest of my family, and to
my parents, Emmanuel and Beatrice.

ACKNOWLEDGEMENTS

I would like to express my deepest and heartfelt appreciation to the following people who have supported me a great deal in writing this dissertation. This has been a huge undertaking and I do not know how I could have made it thus far, without their help.

Words fail me when it comes to describing what the members of my committee have come to mean to me. Dr. Lou D' Abrosca, although you took on the role as my major advisor 'later on', your reassurance and confidence in me kept me focused. You did not only make suggestions, but backed with action and "that has made all the difference"—thank you.

Dr. Clif Boyle, thank you very much for working with me and showing me the big picture. I like your honesty and the pragmatic way you discussed my work. Your relaxed and gentle style assured me I could count on you. Dr. Martin Sivula, I thank you very much for the high expectation you have set for yourself and others like me. You pushed me to work harder and to think and that really kept me on track and helped me a great deal.

Dr. Ronald DiBattista, I would like to thank you for the time you spent with your colleagues in deliberations over my work. I still remember the emails you sent back and forth which clarified certain issues - thank you.

Next, I would like to thank the educational community in Rhode Island, whose names I would have liked to acknowledge but due to assurances of confidentiality, I cannot. You were extremely helpful to me and your willingness to share made this study possible.

To all my friends here in the United States and Ghana, I offer my sincere thanks for your support, help and encouragement. My warmest thanks to my brothers who are all in Ghana for their unconditional love and prayers - it meant a lot.

To my father and mother, I thank you for the premium you placed on education and for your support during the time of my dissertation writing.

To Freda, Kobby and Monique, thanks for understanding all those times when I was too busy to be involved with your lives - and Kobby, for all those basketball games I missed!

Finally, to my husband Joe - how can I thank you for all the sacrifices you made?

Again, words fail me. I leaned a great deal on your support and encouragement and I know I could **not** have written this dissertation **without** you. My deepest and sincere appreciation to you for making this experience a positive one- thanks!

CONTENTS

DEDICATION vii
ACKNOWLEDGEMENTS ix
ABSTRACT xvii

CHAPTER 1: INTRODUCTION 1
Background 2
   The Changing Role of the Secondary School Principal ... 4
   Student Achievement As Influenced by the Principal 10
   Evaluating the Secondary School Principal 10
   Principal Preparation 12
Statement of Problem 13
Purpose of the Study 14
Research Questions 14
Research Question 15
Subquestions 15
Definition of Terms 15
Significance of Study 17
Limitations 17
Delimitations 18
Summary 18

CHAPTER 2: REVIEW OF RELATED LITERATURE 19
Motivation Defined 21
Historical Overview of Motivation 25

Pre Scientific Management Era:
Pre - 1900 Theories of Motivation 25
Early Philosophers 25
   Hedonism 26
   Classification of Motivation Variables 26
   Scientific Management Era: 1900-1930's 27
Studies in the Area of Industrial Psychology 1930's - 1960's 31
Theories of Motivation 32
   Behavioral Theories and Motivation 33
   Cognitive Theories of Motivation 33
   Achievement Motivation 34
   Expectancy x Vahle Theory 35
   Humanistic Theories of Motivation 36
Leadership 38
   Characteristics of Leadership Defined 40
   Historical Overview of Leadership 42
   Human Relations 45
   Social System Theory 47
   Post Modern E:ra 48
Contemporary Leadership Theories 49
   Theory X and Theory Y 50
   TheoryX 51
   Theory Y 52
Behavior Associated with Theory Y 54
   Transformational Leadership 55
The Transformational Leader 56
   Moral Leadership 57
   Empowered Leadership 58
   Conditions for Empowerment 59
   New Roles for Secondary School Principals 60
   Historical Overview of the Principalship 61
   The Current State of the Prindpalship 62
   The State of the Prindpalship 63

    The Principal as Instructional Leader 66
    The Principal's Influence on Student Achievement 70
    Skills Inherent to Successful Principals 72
Development of Principals 75
Phases of Principal Development 78
    Principal Preparation 78
    Alternate Preparation Programs for Principals 79
    Mentoring 80
    Training and Development of Experienced Principals ...82
Summary 84

CHAPTER 3: METHODOLOGY 86
Statement of the Problem 86
Research Questions 86
    Research Question 87
    Subquestions 87
Population and Sample 87
Research Design 88
Instrumentation 90
The Interviewing Process 93
    Introduction 93
    Questioning 94
    Wrap-Up 94
    Questions 95
Data Collection Procedures 95
Data Analysis 95
Summary 98

CHAPTER 4: FINDINGS 100
Introduction 100
Population and Sample 101
Instrumentation 101
    Questions 101
Interview Process 102

Introduction 102
Questioning..102
Wrap - Up 103
Research Findings...103
Research uestion # 1 103
Findings 106
Instructional Leader...106
Organizational Leader 106
Discussion 108
Findings 109
Instructional Leadership 109
Discussion 111
Research Subquestion # 2 111
Findings 114
Principal as Collaborator 114
Principal as Capacity Builder 114
Instructional Leadership 114
Principal as Organizational Leader.............................115
Discussion 115
Forming Strong Connections with Parents and the Community...117
Research Subquestion # 3 117
Findings 120
Discussion 122
Summary...122

CHAPTER 5: SUMMARY, CONCLUSIONS, RECOMMENDATIONS, AND IMPLICATIONS FOR FUTURE RESEARCH 123

Introduction..123
Purpose of the Study 123
Research Design 125
Research Questions..125
Research Question # 1 125

Corroborating Literature 126
Conclusions 128
   Summary of Findings 128
   Research Question # 1 128
   Research Subquestion # 1 129
   Research Subquestion # 2 129
   Research Subquestion # 3 130
Recommendations..131
Implications for Future Research 132

REFERENCES **135**
APPENDICES:
   A. Use of Human Subjects in Field Projects and/or
      Dissertation Research..143
   B. Letter of introduction...147
   C. Consent Form..149
   D. The Evaluation Process 155
   E. The Interview Questions 157
   F. Interstate School Leaders Licensure Consortimn
      (ISLLC Standards) 159

LIST OF TABLES

Table 1: Interview Questions and Corresponding Research Questions 91
Table 2: Data Analysis Matrix Question 97
Table 3: Characteristics that Contribute to the Success of Secondary School Principals 104
Table 4: Characteristics that Contribute to the Success of Secondary School Principals 107
Table 5: Motivation: Emerging Themes 110
Table 6: How do Leadership Styles Contribute to the Development of Successful School Principals 112
Table 7: What are the Factors that Contribute to the Development of Successful Principals? 118
Table 8: Development of Secondary School Principals .. 121

ABSTRACT

This study identifies characteristics that contribute to the success of secondary school principals in the state of Rhode Island. A qualitative research design was employed to determine (a) The impact of motivation on the role relationship of principals, (b) How leadership styles contribute to the success of secondary school principals, and (c) What factors contribute to the professional development of secondary school principals.

While the school sample used in the study was randomly selected, the participants (N = 20) were purposively selected secondary school principals identified as "exemplary educators" by their respective superintendents, and as determined by the respective school district established criteria.

Guided by a qualitative research design, data were collected through individual interviews with each of the twenty principals. Conclusions drawn from the resulting emerging themes suggest that successful principals are visionary instructional leaders who promote student learning and support teachers through collaborative means. In addition, successful principals are self - confident and motivated, and derive much of their professional development from colleagues and through community partnerships.

The results of this study suggest the need for collegial support for principals from various constituencies, as it was determined that an effective principal is critical to the teaching/learning process. Finally, it was determined that the high attrition rate among principals reflects their frustration with ever - increasing expectations thrust upon them, further suggesting the need for professional and moral support for these administrators.

CHAPTER ONE

INTRODUCTION

Across the United States, there is a flourish of activity designed to help school districts meet academic standards. Generally negative views of education are fueled by the publication of test scores in local newspapers (Erickson, 1998) have had a profound effect on education. The emphasis on test results as a criteria for assessing the success of secondary school principals became widespread after the publication of *A Nation at Risk: The Imperative for Educational Reform* (1983).

This publication revealed the low academic performance of some public school students and educators across the country begun to seek reliable methods for raising academic standards.

> The National Commission on Excellence in Education (1983) states that the American people have 'in effect been committing an act of unilateral education disarmament. Our society and its educational institutions seem to have lost sight of the basic purposes of schooling, and of the high expectations and disciplined effort needed to attain them.' (p. 2)

Background

There is no doubt that the poor academic performance of some American public schools lends credence to the assertion, and consequently, the public awareness of this state of affairs has led to near panic among teachers and administrators; hence the high attrition rates among principals. There are many reasons that account for this state of affairs, but researchers have found that a successful principal can bring positive changes in our secondary schools. Therefore, this study focuses on factors that contribute to the success of secondary school principals. The question that has been posed by researchers concerned with the educational system is a perennial one, and that is, what factors make it possible for some secondary school principals to be categorized as successful despite the exhaustive demands placed on them by stakeholders, parents and teachers?

In a recent study using the Myers-Briggs Type Indicator Test, Loos (2001) noted that many constituencies are holding the principals more accountable, forcing them to achieve higher standards in all areas, with less money. Moreover, principals have been called upon to balance their jobs, to build and enhance human relationships. This requires a leadership style that fosters relationships within the school, and between the school and its community. The mission and purposes of schooling are complex and school leaders face many challenges. Indeed, effective principals need both "technical competence and symbolic sensitivity to get the job done with dignity and grace" (Deal & Peterson, 1994, p. 10).

Clearly, the principal's job has also been affected by the pressing need for graduates of American public schools to be able to compete with their counterparts from Europe and the Fareast. According to Erickson (1998), "when the United States had an economy that operated largely on local industry and national corporations, the concern over education was not so pronounced" (p.1). Stakeholders, including parents and students' future employers are looking to principals to produce 'better' schools and well-educated students, who will participate in and contribute to the global economy.

Therefore, this study investigated the role of the principal as it affects student achievement. Further, this study examined the abilities, characteristics and leadership styles of successful principals.

The job of adequate preparation of students, undoubtedly, falls on the school principal as does teacher preparation. Further, this study examined a comprehensive set of factors that contributed to the of secondary school principals, by examining their abilities, characteristics and leadership styles.

A number of studies cite the school principal as the most important catalyst in any successful school (Bookbinder, 1992; Levin, 1997; Lipham, 1981; Sybouts & Wendel, 1994). With respect to the principal's role as a school leader, "it has been viewed much more of an art, a belief, a condition of the heart, than a set of things to do. The visible signs of artful leadership are expressed ultimately in its practice" (De Pree, 1989, p. 11).

Goertz (2000) attempted to establish a relationship between creativity and leadership by conducting a study with a sample of four effective principals from school districts located in the Southwest. These were school districts that participated in the National Association of Secondary School Principals' Center (NASSP, 1978). The findings reveal the current need for creativity traits to be considered a viable component in leadership training. He concluded that effective leadership qualities consist of more than being an administrator or manager.

Effective leadership requires orchestrating the totality of the enterprise with creativity traits of passion for work, independence, and goal setting and original thought processes and creative flexibility. Any leader who is able to work within this paradigm must have a wide range of interests, intelligence, creativity and motivation (Goertz, 2000). It is quite clear that a multiplicity of factors lead to successful principlaship, and this study examined the factors that led to such successes. Apart from being creative, the successful principal is viewed as the lead instructor at the school. This is because the principal should be able to establish a climate for excellence by modeling that behavior. He or she promotes excellence in teaching and learning and commits to sustain professional development for all staff members in order to bring them to the level needed by the district and the state (Tirrozzi, 2001).

The Changing Role of the Secondary School Principal

"These are indeed turbulent times in the American public school system and at a time when strong leadership is needed, most of them are in the least favorable to provide it" (Pullan, 1998, p. 6). As a result of the tremendous pressure that has been placed on principals because of accountability measures, many of them are beginning to review their roles as leaders. The pressure on principals from their many constituencies has led to some form of inertia among principals, because they are not quite sure where to focus their attention. "These are indeed tough times for public educators and many have come to question what they stand for. Many experience an erosion in commitment to whatever that is, and many, one way or the other are giving up" (Pullan, 1997, p. vii).

This state of affairs for the public school principal, accounts for the high shortage of principals nation wide. According to Gilman and Lanman - Givens (2001) "the principal shortage looms, yet fewer candidates are willing to take up the daunting tasks of the principal" (p. 72). The authors invariably blame the shortage on principals' low pay, the pressure of the job, long hours and lack of authority. They therefore suggest that principal preparation programs will have to change to attract more candidates.

Yerkes and Guaglianone (1998) contended that for anyone looking for a job in high school administration, "the prospects look good over the next few years, as more and more districts are reporting shrinking numbers of quality applicants and universities are noticing fewer graduate students interested in working at the secondary school level" (p.10). Yerkes and Guaglianone (1998) reported that conversations they had with colleagues around the nation "coupled with a preliminary study by the *National Association of Elementary and Secondary School Principals* (1998) confirm nationwide applicant shortage" (p.10).

A study conducted by the *Association of California School Administrators* in 1998 with 11 representative school districts revealed that "positions went unfilled for reasons such as stress, salary and a shortage of qualified candidates" (Yerkes & Guaglianone, 1998, pp. 10-14).

Love (2000) conducted a study to find *The Availability of Qualified Candidates for the Secondary Principalship in Arkansas*. The study focused on the availability of qualified candidates for the principalship in Arkansas. The study also addressed factors that encouraged or discouraged applicants in seeking principalship and actions that would attract qualified candidates to the principalship. The sample consisted of the 310 Arkansas public school superintendents, with school districts categorized by student population size and by geographic region of the state. The superintendents had to respond to 25 survey questions.

The study found out that 69% of Arkansas superintendents believed there to be inadequate number of qualified candidates for secondary principalship. Factors that most discouraged qualified applicants were the leadership opportunities available within school districts and the academic reputations of the school districts. In addition, factors that most discouraged qualified applicants were the time commitment for after - school activity supervision and the amount of job - related stress associated with the position.

Another factor that seems to add to the pressure on secondary school principals is the call for them to be leaders of reform movements in education. Secondary school principals are caught within two worlds, they are not sure whether they should lead reform agendas or be managers within their school settings. The idea of a principal being both a principal and a manager in the true sense of the word, has made the job extremely complex (Fullan, 1998, Sybouts & Wendel, 1994).

In order to establish the transition that has taken place within the principalship and the complexity of the job, Johnson (1993) conducted a study relating to *The Principal and School Effectiveness.* The study attempted to establish relationships between organizational effectiveness and the effectiveness of organizational leaders. The sample was made up of 112 elementary school principals in Alberta Canada. The results support a close relationship between the two constructs and highlight the complexity of educational leadership.

Most scholars will agree that the nature of the principalship has changed tremendously and Sybouts and Wendel (1994) supported this assertion. They contended that

> A gradual transition has taken place as schools have grown in size and complexity, and the principalship has gone from a position in management and control to one that demands

instructional leadership. In modem schools, the demands on persons in the principal's position are becoming more complex than ever before because of the pluralism and the complexity of society itself." (Sybouts & Wendel, 1994, p. 13)

As middle managers, principals would also have to be able to maintain rapport with teachers as well as those in the hierarchy. Sometimes principals are forced to spearhead and promote initiatives they have no hand in developing, and this creates additional overload and tension for secondary school principals.

As a result of the national shortage of secondary school principals due to the mass exodus from the profession, researchers are beginning to examine new roles for the secondary school principal. Goldering and Rallis (1993) explored the idea of how principals' assumption of new roles of principals will shape their leadership, and the following ideas emerged from their work. They believed that that there were certain forces that shaped the activities of the secondary school principals. For example, teachers are assuming more active roles and becoming teacher - leaders, parents are also becoming more vocal in school affairs and student bodies are also more diverse.

Since teachers, students and parents are now forces to reckon with in the school systems, one of the new roles of principals, is for them to be able to empower these constituents to be leaders. Short (1998) contended that "teachers and students must become empowered to be active participants in educational improvement and school decision making." A principal who is able to give some of his or her power away by empowering other school personnel, becomes very successful. Short (1998) agreed that "empowered schools and their principals are very different from schools with little empowerment and they also accept responsibilities for their decisions" (p. 70). The difference lies in the energy and the positive environment that the empowered individuals create. These teachers, parents and students feel that they have ownership within the school and that idea encourages them to push their school's reform agenda toward success.

There is also no doubt that the student body is becoming more diverse and sometimes very challenging to school officials. As cited earlier in this study, the poor performance of some of our public school students has led to state and federal mandates to various school districts. All these factors have become very important in the daily operations of the school principal and this implies that the school leader will also have to take on a new role of working smoothly with all these constituents. The principal will have to be an active listener, facilitator, flag bearer, communicator, a and a visionary (Goldring & Rallis, 1993; Smith & Andrews, 1989).

In relation to the new roles of secondary school principals, Guzman (1997) describes a multiple case analysis of six elementary school principals considered to be successful leaders of inclusive schools. The researcher discovered that each principal established an open communication system, was actively involved in the development of *Individualized Educational Plans* for students, personally conversed with parents of disabled students.

The actions of these principals support the notion that successful principals for the current school systems, will need a paradigm shift in their actions and thinking. They can no longer be the 'Lone Ranger' type who attempts to solve all problems, but rather individuals who are in constant communication with their stakeholders. In fact,

Strodl (1993) stipulated that the degree to which constituent groups participate in school activities goes a long way to determine the quality of teaching and learning that goes on in the school. Strodl (1993) again agreed that in order for the principal to do this effectively, he or she must be very intuitive, sensitive, should be able to gather information effectively, and be able explore alternatives to problems very quickly.

The principal who assumes this new role should also be able to provide the needed professional development support and resources to attain academic goals, having a profound understanding of the curriculum and innovative instructional practices so that he or she can move forward the reform agenda relating to teaching and learning. The issue that seems to plaque that minds of educators and other stake holders, is whether principal preparation programs are preparing school leaders to assume these new roles?

There are studies to demonstrate that leaders who assume these new roles, will ultimately improve the performance and achievement of his or her students. Silins (1994) conducted a study which investigated the relationship between school principals' leadership behaviors and school outcomes in a Canadian school involved in reform efforts. Results indicate transformational leadership behaviors were more effective than transactional leadership styles in promoting teacher, program, instructional and student outcomes.

This study firmly supports the importance of leadership in effective school reform. Since the involvement of the school principal in school reform will enhance teaching and learning, it is expected that one of the avenues for principals to achieve this goal, will be to have direct influence on instruction through professional development activities, modeling, coaching an teaching (Hart & Bredson, 1996).

Student Achievement As Influenced by the Principal

As previously cited, secondary school principals are supposed to assume the role of instructional leaders and it is therefore not surprising that for the most part, they are held accountable for the achievement of their students. Ewing (2001) conducted a study on accountable leadership and he tried to determine a relationship between the leadership style of a principal and student achievement

The study surveyed 50 principals and 75 teachers from high - middle and

Low - achieving elementary public schools in Chicago. Leadership styles were defined according to Blanchard's Model of Situational Leadership II. The findings indicated that situational leadership styles of the principals were significantly related to student achievement in reading and mathematics. If in fact a principal's role in school reform can influence students' performance, then principals can be held accountable for student achievement, which invariably means that students' performance can become part of the evaluation process of the principal.

Evaluating the Secondary School Principal

In many school systems, the responsibilities of evaluating the principals fall on the shoulders of the superintendent. In larger school systems however, the task is beyond the capacity of one individual (Franklin, 2000). Thus, the way principals are evaluated also poses a problem because depending on what system is used, a principal who is seen as unsuccessful by one system could be deemed as 'successful' in another. Rallis and Goldring (1993) discussed forces that are changing principals' roles and they explore the implications of the new roles for principal evaluation. They also suggest that "evaluation should include individual and school - based components following the ways in which work and tasks are organized in dynamic schools" (p. 3).

Many educators are looking for reliable method and standard by which school leaders could be evaluated. This search has become necessary because many educators believe that it is not fair that the performance of a secondary school principal is judged by the performance of his or her students on standardized tests. For example, within the old paradigm, one school system went as far as to base 65% of a principal's evaluation on students' test score (Franklin, 2000).

It has become evident that students' test scores have become a force to reckon with when it comes to a principal's evaluation, and that poses a problem. This method of assessment is problematic because principals feel they do not have control over all the variables involved in standardized testing and this adds to the pressure they feel on the job. Many researchers feel that the premise for evaluating principals by test scores is flawed and the whole idea needs to be evaluated.

Through a close examination of the problem, Franklin (2000) found that the systems for evaluating teachers **are** much better and systematic in most cases than they are for evaluating principals. In fact, some states do not have legislation that provides guidance in what will be evaluated or suggested models which could be used for evaluation (Reed, 2000). This means that secondary school principals in many states are not evaluated by clear and uniformed standards.

This ambiguity has left some of these principals in doubt, thereby, adding to their frustration, since for the most part they are not sure if they are being evaluated fairly and equitably. Thus, in an attempt to find a common ground for principal evaluation, Rhode Island and other states have turned to the Interstate School Leaders Licensure Consortium (ISLLC Standards). The Consortium was established in 1994, and it developed its standards in 1996. The consistency which the ISLLC Standards provide, experts say, is essential for reforming the way some principal evaluations are conducted. The ISLLC Standards afford principals the opportunity to be reflective in their practice because the consortium vision of leadership is grounded in the knowledge and understanding of teaching and learning (ISLLC Standards, 2000).

There is no doubt that if principal evaluation is authentic, it could become a tool for assessing principals' needs. Such needs assessment could influence preparation of school principals because the way principals are prepared unequivocally leads to how they perform on the job. Therefore, the factor worth examining at this point is,

Principal Preparation

With the overwhelming and growing responsibilities of the secondary school principal, researchers continue to study the preparation of school leaders for this high accountability job. This has become necessary because researchers are beginning to wonder if a change in principal preparation will raise the quality of school leadership (Keller, 2000). To help alleviate the current crisis in the principalship, there is a move throughout the United States to provide a network of support and information for leadership in educational administration and new principals (Licata, Joseph, Elliot & Chad, 1990).

Other factors that have led to change in principal preparation, include the reports issued about the conditions of public schools. "The reports on conditions of education in the United States that were issued during the decade of the 1980's impacted heavily upon the method of preparing educational administrators by citing the inadequate training these professionals were receiving at the colleges and universities" (Earthman, 1990, p. 1).

In the late 1980's, the situation was so grave, that the *National Commission on Excellence in Educational Administration,* suggested closing over three hundred administrator - training programs in more than three hundred institutions of higher learning (Stover, 1990). A multiplicity of factors were listed for this dismal state of affairs and among them were the following: quality candidates, minorities, clinical experiences and irrelevant course work (Earthman, 1990, Stover, 1990).

Since principal preparation has been identified as one of the contributing factors to the current crisis in the principalship, researchers are attempting to find alternate routes to principal preparation and certification. Researchers have suggested that the development of leadership, can be fostered by coaching and mentorship through networks or within study groups (Mann, 1990).

Many school districts have taken these suggestions seriously, and have developed plans to initiate support systems for administrators and these include the following: (a) Developing a personal support system, (b) Increased administrator performance, (c) Development of instructional leadership skills, (d) Networking, (e) Collegial problem solving and (f) Establishing the forum for discussion (Daresh & Playko, 1992; Rogus & Drury, 1988).

Statement of Problem

Since successful schools seem to be dependent on their principals (United States Department of Education, 1996; Bookbinder, 1992; Sybouts & Wendel, 1994), it is necessary to identify and assess the degree to which various factors contribute to the success of secondary school principals.

Purpose of the Study

There has been a renewed interest in the performance of public schools since the publication of the *A Nation at Risk* (1983). This renewed interest in education has led to an abundance of research focused on effective schools, characteristics and skills of effective principals, and leadership. In fact, a number of studies identify the principal as the critical element in successful schools (Bookbinder, 1992; Levin,1997; Lipham, 1981; Sybouts & Wendel, 1994).

Therefore, this study investigated the factors that contribute to the success of secondary school principals. Specifically, the study reviewed the impact of various factors in terms of their contribution to the success of secondary school principals. These factors include mentoring, training and development programs, alternate routes to certification, and personal reflection through the use of the Interstate School Leaders Licensure Consortium (ISLLC Standards).

Research Questions

The primary research question of this study was designed by incorporating major findings from the literature review: (a) Characteristics of Successful Principals, (b) The hnpact of Motivation on the Role Relationship of principals, (c) Leadership Styles and (d) Development of Successful Principals. In order to come to an understanding as to why some principals are successful, the following questions were addressed in the course of the study and the literature review.

Research Question

What are the characteristics that contribute to the success of secondary school principals?

Subquestions

(1) What is the impact of motivation on the role relationship of principals?
(2) How do leadership styles contribute to the development of successful principals?
(3) What factors contribute to the development of principals' success?

Definition of Terms

Development - Training, development, and other strategies that contribute to the learning and growth of an individual. For example, it can be any type of assistance given to a student to ensure that the student reaches his or her full academic development in reading and writing.

Effective Schools - Schools identified as successful in meeting established criteria as determined by educational research.

Evaluation - A method of assessing whether a principal is effective or not.

Instmctional Leader - A specific role and responsibility of the principalship which is focused on enhancing student achievement; curriculum development and implementation, strong instructional practices, and assessing student learning.

ISLLC - Interstate School Leaders Licensure Consortium: In the past, standards for licensing school administrators were complex and varied widely. This instrument was developed to ensure that the process for evaluating principals' work is unified and streamlined. The alliance involves thirty educational agencies and thirteen education administrative associations including the Association for Supervision and Curriculum Development.

Leadership - The ability to elicit a fellowship, the ability to involve others, empower others, and interact with individuals as well as with groups. Leadership will be measured according to how a particular institution defines leadership and then an appropriate test will be developed to measure that particular requirement.

Leadership Assessment Program - A leadership program that provides information on personal strengths and areas for growth potential.

Manager - A specific role and responsibility of the principalship in which the principal performs management skills including planning, organizing, staffing, directing and controlling.

Mentor - A trusted advisor who engages with a colleague in a way that provides support, teaching and learning relative to the craft.

Principal - The highest level position within a school organization from grades seven to twelve This individual communicates directly with the central office administration, and is responsible for carrying out new initiatives and reforms as stated by the school district. In addition, they are also considered as building managers.

Successful Schools - Schools identified as successful in meeting established criteria determined by educational research and also as defined by state and national guidelines.

Transformational Leadership - The ability for people in the organization to engage with each other in a way that elevates them to higher levels of motivation and self - actualization.

Two Factor Theory of Motivation - A theory of motivation in which there are two independent sets of factors that contribute to human motivation; intrinsic, and extrinsic.

Significance of Study

The literature about school leadership is plentiful and covers more than three decades. Yet, the research particular to the state of Rhode Island is limited. Moreover, since there is a renewed interest in leadership in secondary schools, it is intended that the findings from this study will have particular significance for school districts, educational leaders, administrators, and governing boards.

It is further expected that findings from this study will inform principal preparation, induction, and continued potential development programs. Specifically, the findings for this study will inform policy making, drafting procedures for improving the principalship, and further research.

Limitations

The following limitations were identified in the study: The purposive sampling of 20 secondary school principals decreased the generalizability of this study to other secondary school principals in other states. In addition, qualitative research methods call into question subjective misunderstandings in the interpretation of findings. Moreover, the researcher is an educator within the state being investigated, which could arise potential bias. Finally, volunteers could have differed from non-volunteers which could compromise interpretation and mitigate against generalizbility of the results (Isaac & Michael, 1995).

Delimitations

This study was limited to secondary school principals in Rhode Island, and also to only one type of research design (exploratory study), using audio - taped interviews with informed consent from each participant.

Summary

The principal is the most important individual in a given school. A number of factors have influenced the secondary school principalship, and its current complex nature requires individuals with a varied sense about life and leaders who are willing to respond to trends that educational constituencies present. Therefore, it is important to investigate the factors that contribute to the success of secondary school principals, in order to inform principal preparation, induction, and professional development programs.

CHAPTER TWO

REVIEW OF RELATED LITERATURE

Chapter Two investigated Motivation, Leadership, Leadership Styles, Characteristics of successful Principals, and the Development of Successful Principals.

A review of the literature revealed that these domains are critical to successful leadership. This chapter therefore, defines motivation, explores the theory of motivation, and identifies the ability to motivate as an important quality of any successful leader, especially, that of the secondary school principal. This discussion will help to answer the question "what is the impact of motivation on the role relationship of principals?"

Various leadership theories were also explored and a relationship was identified between the leadership theories and the early theories of motivation. The research revealed that leadership theories such as transformational leadership moral leadership and empowerment are based on the premise that the leader and the follower self - actualize.

The ensuing relationship established between principals and teachers informs agendas and fosters a sense of empowerment.

Various leadership styles are also examined in this chapter, especially as it pertains to the leadership of secondary school principals. Since there is a preponderance of literature on leadership styles, the researcher explored the idea behind Theory Y and Theory X because the way a principal views his or her staff members goes a long way to determine the success of that principal.

Next, research about successful principals was reviewed for three reasons. First, it is closely linked with the research on leadership in that an effective principal must be a leader who collaborates and also develops leadership qualities in others. Secondly, the literature about successful principals indicates that the ability to motivate teachers and students to engage in meaningful reforms will lead to achievement.

The researcher also explored the body of literature which focused on specific skills that principals need in order for them to be successful. Such skills are developed through, authentic, appropriate, and timely professional development. A national priority, engaging principals in continuous learning through mentoring, reflection, support systems and other means will contribute to their success in a particularly critical and difficult role.

Motivation is a theory that seems to be inextricably linked to any form of leadership, so in examining the factors that contribute to successful secondary school principals, the following headings will be explored: Motivation Defined; Historical Overview of Motivation; and the Theories of Motivation and lastly; the Summary.

As a result of the vastness of the literature about motivation, a section of this literature review was attributed to problems with defining motivation.

The second main heading, historical overview of motivation was developed with a review of pre 1900 theories of motivation. The review followed the evolution of the motivation through the scientific management era, and human relations era.

The third heading, theories of motivation was a presentation of behavioral, cognitive, and humanistic perspectives of motivation theories. A synthesis of the various theories was provided and then the researcher connected the major concept of the theory of motivation to that of successful principalship.

Motivation Defined

Webb and Norton (1999) stated that education is related to the social, political and economic influences of its time, thus viewed as the microcosm of the society. They further explained that "a major responsibility of the human resources function is maximizing the human resources of the school system. It is essential, therefore, that human resources administrators understand the basic concept of human motivation as they relate to maximizing human resources" (p. 337). One aspect of education requires individuals to teach or to learn. However, motivation is not limited to education and its definition should be viewed through different lenses.

For example, to the economist, motivation could mean appropriate use of money to encourage people to work harder if linked to good performance. "The industrial psychologist focuses on the basic needs and expectations of the members of the enterprise and the extent to which those needs are being satisfied by the particular organizational circumstances under consideration" (Hindrichs, 1974, p. 38). Both cognitive perspective and the humanistic perspectives view motivation as intrinsic, or arising from within the individual (Owens, 1998).

Another definition offered is that, "motivation deals with explanations of why people do the things they do for millennia, the mysteries of why people behave as they do has fascinated dramatists, artists, writers, composers, philosophers social scientists and theologians" (Owens, 1995, p. 24). It is in the understanding of this definition of motivation that one notes the important role of the secondary school principal. For example, what skills do successful principals embrace in order to motivate the people in their constituencies, to engage in the activities that make the school successful and hence, deem the principal also successful?

Initial research on the topic of motivation begun within the decade between 1890-1900, and a large number of studies were conducted between 1900 to the 1960's. Many scholars have presented extensive work on motivation (Lopez, 1998). Among them is Madsen (1961) who presented the work of twenty theorists whose studies focused on the topic of motivation. It is quite clear that to present one definition to cover all aspects of motivation may be nearly impossible. The problems that arise with the definition of motivation lie with the following: (a) The many fields of inquiry in the behavioral sciences and psychology studying and attempting to define motivation, (b) The extensive and multiplicity of proposed theories of motivation. (c) The multitude of variables under the same heading, and (d) A variety of languages that have been used in describing motivation (Lopez, 1998).

The fields of inquiry are numerous but have attempted to define motivation within their own parameters or disciplines of study. Psychologists who are mostly interested in the testing aspect, develop, administer, interpret and redefine tests for individual differences. In career guidance for example, counselors can administer career inventory tests in order to suggest a career for a particular personality traits. An example of such a test is the Myers-Briggs Type Indicator Test or David Kiersey's personality test.

Sometimes, psychologists administer these tests in order to pick out the right personnel for a particular job or situation. "To them, motivation is what is referred to be the test the measurement of individual differences in motivation is conceived of as the discovery of how individuals differ in what they like and dislike" (Atkinson & Birch, 1978, p. 9).

Clinical psychologists define motivation in terms of interrelationships between unconscious thoughts and behavior (Atkinson & Birch, 1978). Since they deal with the relational aspect of the human being, they tend to be more involved in the counseling aspect of psychology.

The second problem with the definition of motivation is the "numerous theories that have been propounded by different researchers" (Webb & Norton, 1999, p. 339). "Some theories center on outcome behaviors that are influenced by individuals' perceptions of past events and/ or how they perceive future outcomes relative to their personal needs and beliefs. Other theories view behavior as "an action that can be changed through interventions that modify an individual's responses" (Webb & Norton, 1999 p. 339) "The terms "behavior modification," "drive - reinforcement theory", "operant conditioning" and "behaviorism" all generally relate to the concept that the behavior of an individual can be altered or changed through the appropriate intervention" (Webb & Norton, 1999, p. 339).

The third problem with defining motivation is that many variables that have been used for testing theories and for interpreting data, which makes defining motivation a formidable task. As cited in this study, motivation has been defined in a number of ways by performing a number of different functions, and it is quite a challenge to define motivation to include all these terms and variables.

The final problem with the definition of motivation lies in the very fact that it is a theory that is embraced by all disciplines of life and academics, hence, each discipline expresses the idea of motivation with their own language. These many languages, terms, and phrases used make it very difficult to design an inclusive definition of motivation. In fact, the issue about motivation is so controversial that there is much disagreement among scholars about the different theories of motivation (Owen, 1998). Nonetheless,

Atkinson, and Birch (1978) and Owens (1995) presented a broad definition of motivation. They defined motivation as the ability to enhance the understanding of human nature. To support the above assertion, Owens, (1998), posed the following question:

> For example, why do some teachers come to work and do as little as is necessary, whereas others are full of energy and ideas and throw themselves zealously into the job? Why do some principals seem to focus on the day to day operations in the school with no apparent vision of where the school should be headed, whereas others seem to embrace a clear, coherent vision of the school as it ought to be and pursue it consistently over the course of the years? (Owens, 1999, p., 118)

One issue that was considered in this study was whether the success of a secondary school principal is dependent upon their ability to motivate teachers, students, parents and other staff members to believe in a particular reform or initiative. Another issue is if the principal' s ability to motivate, changes the negative attitude of some of the members of his constituency, especially teachers, thereby leading to his or her success.

Historical Overview of Motivation

Pre Scientific Management Era:
Pre - 1900 Theories of Motivation

A review of the literature revealed that motivation has been of great interest in many fields and disciplines. The Pre-Scientific Era and the work of early philosophers generated the concept of hedonism (Lopez, 1998). Research conducted between 1900- 1930 such as the Western Electric Studies, had a tremendous impact on our understanding of motivation during this period. Some of the most significant research was conducted at the beginning of the Scientific Management Era through the Human Relations Era. The research conducted during this era focused on the behavioral, cognitive and also the humanistic aspect of education. This research is very important to the field of education because it examined with human needs, growth and development, and personal achievement. We can therefore ask, how can a principals knowledge of human needs and development affect his or her leadership styles and thereby leading to successful principalship?

Early Philosophers

Early interests and attempts to study motivation were recorded by well-known philosophers such as Aristotle and Thomas Acquinas. "Aristotle and other philosophers of antiquity have described 'desire' or 'drives' as one of the 'mental forces' or 'abilities' on par with others such as perceptions, imagination, and feeling" (Madsen, 1961, p. 64). The concept of Hedonism also came into existence between the 18th and 19th century.

Hedonism

Some of the modern motivational theories have their origins in the philosophy of Hedonism which was started by the English Utilitarians, Jeremy Bentam and John Stuart Mill. The notion of hedonism is based on the idea that people's behavior can be explained in terms of achieving pleasure and avoiding pain. The idea of Hedonism was later expanded by William James in the late 1800's (Atkinson & Birch, 1978; Madsen, 1961; Porter, 1968).

Classification of Motivation Variables

There were many attempts to classify motivation variables during the pre-1900's. William Wendt who was the originator of experimental psychology, substantiated the two variables of motivation (emotion and will) and believed that there was a close relationship between the two. William James also espoused the idea that "man had the most instincts and that these instincts impacted the will and other psychologists regarded "instincts" as the essential motives for behavior (Madsen, 1961, p. 44).

Through the work of Sigmund Freud (1856-1939), it was discovered that instincts and drives were of primary importance in people's behavior and development. Freud explained virtually all behaviors by referring to manifestations of unconscious personality processes, and he concluded that "the dethronement of consciousness as the locus of determinants of human activity" (Atkinson & Birch, 1978, p. 12).

Understanding behavior therefore, required a careful scrutiny of personality to determine the meaning of behavior (Kazdin, 1994). This information is important to the research question "what factors contribute to the success of secondary school principals" because schools are influenced by people and relationships. The question becomes, is the successful principal the individual who is able to tap into the human capital available to him or her at his or here school?

Scientific Management Era: 1900-1930's

It is common place for students of education to learn about the Hawthorne Effect, also known as the Western Electric Studies. This classic research is one of the most significant of its era, and has led to a more comprehensive understanding of motivation at work (Owens, 1998). An experimental study that begun in 1924 and ended ten years later, was conducted at the Hawthorne Works of the Western Electric Company, located in Cicero near Chicago (Owens ,1998 p. 122).

The purpose of this Western Electric Study was to find out how much illumination was required to achieve the maximum output from workers. Two groups of employees doing similar work under similar conditions were selected as the sample for this study. The results of the study showed that the experimental group of workers responded to the 'perceptions' of the researchers' expectations. Thus, the workers were responding to psychological factors that motivated their behavior at work (Owens, 1998), hence, establishing a relationship between productivity and psychological factors.

After the study on the relationship between illumination and productivity was concluded, a new experimental study was organized in the Hawthorne Works involving workers who assembled telephone relays (Owens, 1998). The researchers used a control group, which worked in the regular shop, and an experimental group, which was given a separate area. Working methodically for a year, the researchers kept careful production records while trying different experimental interventions: rest pauses, special lunch periods, a shorter working day, and a shorter working week.

The central findings of the study are as follows:

(1) The workers liked the experimental situation and considered it fun.
(2) The new form of supervision (encouraging them to work at **a** normal pace and not trying to hurry) made it possible for them to work freely.
(3) The workers knew that what they did was important and that results were expected.
(4) The workers were consulted about planned changes, often by the superintendent himself, and during that process were encouraged to express their views and were in fact, permitted to veto some ideas before they were implemented.
(5) As a result, the group itself had changed and developed during the course of the experiment. Though the last step of the experiment was an attempt to return the group to the original conditions of work by taking away the experimental rest periods, new hours and the like, it was in fact impossible to return the group to its original state because the group had transformed (Owens, 1998, p. 124).

The major impact of the Western Electric studies is that "it set the stage for the evolution of widespread research seeking to better understand the nature and needs of human beings at work and to apply this knowledge to the development of more effective organizations" (Owens, 1998, p. 125). Also, the results showed that the higher productivity achieved during the Western Electric studies was due to cohesiveness, higher morale, and values that were highly motivating, thereby demonstrating the power of team work. "Though school boards, school administrators, and managers who view themselves as being tough, failed for decades to understand the power and significance of this simple and crucial discovery even as it was being confirmed in study after study over the years, it eventually emerged in the 1980's as the central idea in the transformation of organizational life and leadership in the U.S. business and industry and, eventually, education" (Owens, 1998, p. 126). Human Relations E:ra: 1930's - 1960's

According to Webb and Norton (1999) "as early as 1920, the scientific management approach was being brought into question" (p. 43). Webb and Norton (1999) further noted that one of the first personnel textbooks written for industry was authored by Tead and Metcalf (1920) who contended that

> The new focus in administration is to be the human element. The new center of attention and solitude is the individual person, the worker. And this change comes about fundamentally for no sentimental reasons, but because the enlistment of human cooperation, of the interest and goodwill of the workers has become the crux of the production problem. The human approach to effective production administration is through a specialized administrative agency-through the operation of a separate staff department in management... (p. 1)

Thus, the human relations era was conceived-the scientific management era was now viewed as inhumane and it evoked the concern of many writers (Webb & Norton, 1999). Webb and Norton (1999) contended that Follet's

(1924) work was significant as it showed the importance of the human element in an organization. Follet, (1924) based her concepts on managers at work and she set forth a philosophy opposing scientific management. She contended that organizations should not be viewed as inanimate entities, but rather they should seen as systems that embodied the lives of the people who work within it (Follet, 1924). In a series of papers and in her book, *Creative Experience,* she emphasized the need to consider the human element and social ethics in administration.

Mary Parker Follet "was one of the primary founders of the human relations movement in educational administration and she stressed that one of management's primary responsibilities was to establish positive working relationships with workers" (Webb & Norton, 1999, p. 44). The Western Electric Studies made great contributions to the new understanding about motivation in the work place, there were also great strides made in the field of behavioral science and the psychology that emerged.

Many studies were conducted in the area of industrial psychology and they focused mainly on employee needs and attitudes. It is along this domain that secondary school leaders can become resource personnel by performing needs assessments on staff members in order to provide them with the resources they need so that they can become better at teaching. One of the most important studies conducted at this time was Abraham Maslow's Hierarchy of Needs Theory.

Owens (1998) contended that "One of the most powerful and enduring ways of understanding human motivation was developed by Abraham Maslow who unlike the experimental psychologists of his day, decided to study the motivation patterns shown by people as they lived" (Owens, 1998, p. 142). Maslow believed that "people were driven from within to realize their full growth potential. This ultimate goal is sometimes called self-fulfillment, sometimes called self-realization but Maslow called it self-actualization" (Owens, 1998, p. 142).

Maslow believed that "as the need for safety is met, one seeks affiliation: belonging, acceptance by others, and love. Once an individual's need for affiliation are adequately met, one is motivated by the next higher need in the hierarchy, the need for self-esteem: this comes from recognition and respect from others" (Owens, 1998,

p. 142). This invariably means a teacher who feels unsafe in school is not going to be motivated by the new initiatives introduced by the principal of the school. In that case, what will happen to a secondary school principal who has a school filled with unmotivated teachers? How can this principal be successful?

Studies in the Area of Industrial Psychology 1930's - 1960's

Other researchers have tried to examine the style of leadership and its effect on group life goals, behavior, responses and motivation. (Lewin, Lippet &White, 1939) conducted a study looking at responses and motivational levels when being supervised by an autocratic, democratic and laissez- faire leaders. Findings from this study indicated that aggression occurred thirty times and hostility eight times more frequently within a group when an autocratic style is used (Lewin, Lippet & White, 1939).

Another study by Coch and French (1948) investigated a study on the impact of job changes on production workers and their outputs. Results of these experiments indicated that "management can remove resistance to job changes by using group meetings in which management effectively communicates the need for change and stimulates group participation in planning changes" (Coch & French, 1948, p. 581).

> The work of Frederick Herzberg began to appear some 12 years after Maslow's theory had become widely influential in management thought around the world particularly in profit-making organizations. Herzberg started with systematic studies of people at work, thereby producing an empirically grounded theory. (Owens, 1998, p. 148)

The purpose of Herzberg's study was to "recall the circumstances in which (a) Employees had at specific times in the past felt satisfied with their jobs, and in which (b) They similarly had been dissatisfied with their jobs" (Owens, 1998, p. 148). "An analysis of the responses shows that "there is one specific, describable cluster or group of factors that is associated with motivation and satisfaction at work another, an equally specific group of factors that is associated with dissatisfaction and apathy" (Owens, 1998, p.148). We can therefore ask what steps can a secondary school principal take to ensure that he or she understands the real issue being presented by the teachers in the school in order not to confuse maintenance issues with motivational factors?

After defining and tracing the history of motivation from the pre - scientific management era, the scientific management era, human relations era to studies in the area of industrial psychology, it became necessary to examine the theories of motivation as a discipline in its own right.

Theories of Motivation

Research in the area of motivation has been categorized into three main areas, beginning with the extrinsic or behaviorist views, whereby managers sought to motivates individuals with a carrot and stick (Owens, 1998). The other theories are seen as intrinsic, springing from within the individual and these make the cognitive and the humanistic domains (Owens, 1998). In other words, the internal capacities can be motivating or demotivating.

Behavioral Theories and Motivation

As cited earlier, managers who believed in the theory of "behaviorism" found that "people who were hurt tend to move in order to avoid pain and people who are rewarded tend to repeat the behavior that brought them reward" (Owens, 1998, p. 120). The idea of rewarding individuals through the manipulation of positive reinforcers has been widely used in educational organizations. Examples of motivational concepts used in education include merit pay plans, demands for accountability, formal supervision, annual performance reviews tied to reappointment to a position and 'teacher recognition days' (Owens, 1998).

Cognitive Theories of Motivation

A cognitive perspective about motivation is founded on the theory that human beings have an innate inner drive to understand the world, to make sense of it, to gain control over their lives, and to become increasingly self-directed (Owens, 1998). This idea explains why certain individuals are driven to work toward these ends. That is, people tend to be motivated by the need for ordered predictability, sensibleness and logic in dealing with the world (Owens, 1998).

Achievement Motivation

Studies in the area of Achievement motivation began with the work of McCllend, *The Achievement Motive* (Weiner, 1974). Before McClleland's work, there had been various attempts to define achievement motives. This aspect of motivation has been defined qualitatively, but there was a problem when it comes to explaining test results and findings. A rather significant development which helped in determining ahievement motivation, was the Thematic Appreciation Test (TAT) designed to assess strengths of individual needs (Weiner, 1974). Researchers conducted studies and applied the TAT to determine "how individuals differ in disposition to strive for certain goals" (Atkinson & Raynor, 1974, p. 4). The idea resulting from this study are two fold, and they are the following: (a) Individuals drive toward success and avoidance of failure (low achievement), and (b) Individuals avoidance of success and avoidance of failure (high avoidance) (Owens, 1995).

Weber's research during this period also established a relationship between high achievement motivation as a sociocultural norm and his observation during the Belle Epoch led to his work on *The Protestant Ethic and the Spirit of Capitalism* (Owens, 1998). The premise of Weber's thinking was based on the fact that there was a difference between the productivity and the economic development between European Protestant countries and European Roman Catholic countries. Weber's observation led to the fact that the 'protestant ethic' with its emphasis on individual faith and independence and belief in hard work accounted for much of the difference (Owens, 1998). It is clear however, that the research that was carried out by McClelland ties into the idea of Protestantism. Along the same lines, educators have tried to establish a relationship between socioeconomic class and work ethic and student achievement. Thus, the issue that will relate to this study is how can a principal increase the cultural capital of his or her students which could lead to great gains in student achievement?

Expectancy x Vahle Theory

A particular theory of motivation that has influenced motivational psychology is Expectancy x Value Theory. There are three basic tenets of this theory. The first tenet contends that when individuals expect success, the more positive the incentive (affective) value of the goal. In the same manner, the likelihood of failure and the negative incentive value of the goal, the more intense motivation to avoid the goal (Weiner, 1974).

The second idea of the Expectancy x Value Theory is that people maintain expectations regarding particular outcomes. "The terms, reinforcement, value, reward value, utility, and goal demand describe the concept that people have preferences among outcomes" (Porter & Lawler, 1968, p. 10). The issue worth considering at this point is whether a successful secondary principal is the individual who explores the value system of teachers and other staff members and uses them as a form of reward?

A third aspect of Expectancy x value Theory is the idea of a relationship or manipulative factor. In this case, "the expectancy theory of motivation is based on the on the proposition that effort, performance, and rewards are inextricably related. This concept of motivation argues that effort and performance depend on individual's perceptions of their potential for meeting personal reward outcomes" (Webb & Norton, 1999, p. 340).

Humanistic Theories of Motivation

The cognitive perspective on motivation is that we are motivated from within to make sense of the world as we perceive it, to exercise control of our lives, and to be directed from within. The humanistic perspective stipulates that personal needs to constantly grow and develop, to cultivate personal self-esteem, and to have satisfying human relationships are highly motivating drives (Owens, 1998).

Humanistic theories of motivation seek to understand need and values in relation to behavior. There is a continuous quest for growth, development and achievement of the individual's potential. Theories that follow this type of reasoning include Maslow's Hierarchy of Needs Theory and Herzberg's Two Factor Theory of Motivation.

Maslow's theory is grounded in the idea that people are driven intrinsically in the direction of growth, development, and self-fulfillment. The genius of Maslow's work "lies in the hierarchy of needs: that human needs start with survival, then unfold in an orderly, sequential hierarchical pattern that takes us toward continuous growth and development" (Owens, 1998, p. 142). According to Maslow, these basic needs arrange themselves in a fairly definite hierarchy on the basis of how important the need is to the individual Maslow, 1954).

Maslow, also contended that one cannot be motivated to achieve higher order needs if they are deficient in basic physiological needs like food, water, shelter and others in the same category. Maslow further argued that the highest level of need attainment is self-actualization-where one is able to develop into what one is capable of becoming, autonomous and self-directed (Maslow, 1954).

This state of Maslow's theory calls for individuals to develop to their full potential of strengths, abilities, abilities and talents. The call in education is the same. Teachers are being called upon to teach to their best abilities and students are encouraged to learn to their best potential. The critical issue here is for the principal to motivate all his or her constituencies so that these goals can be achieved. With respect to teachers, principals will have to pay more attention to higher level needs such as professional growth and development, achievement and self - actualization. Individuals at the higher levels of the hierarchy are less concerned with survival issues; healthier and biologically efficient; prone to happiness and inner peace; awareness of civic and social responsibilities; less egocentric and more concerned about others; and moving toward individualism (Maslow, 1954).

The work of Frederick Herzberg and his Two Factor Theory of Motivation appeared twelve years after the work of Abraham Maslow. The Two Factor Theory was different from the Hierarchy of Needs because it featured two separate and independent criteria, motivational and maintenance factors which were non-hierarchical in nature.

Herzberg's research involved asking people about specific indications when they felt satisfied with their jobs and similarly, he also asked them to recall occasions when they felt dissatisfied with their jobs.

Herzberg classified the content factors (satisfiers) as: achievement; recognition; work itself; responsibility; and growth and advancement. These satisfiers or content factors were also called motivators, which because of its intrinsic nature, brought out the best in people. In the late 1960's, Thomas Sergiovanni replicated Herzberg's work among teachers, and found that the theory appeared to be supported. He contended that achievement and recognition were very important motivators for teachers, "along with the work it self, responsibility, and the possibility of growth" (Owens, 1998, p.152).

Many researchers have compared Maslow's and Herzberg's theories of motivation and have found them to be highly compatible. While Maslow's theory is hierarchical and addresses important needs, Herzberg's theory focuses on the higher needs as motivators. The most important aspect of these studies is that they both dwell on the needs of the individual as a means of attaining motivation.

Leadership

Leadership has been defined in several ways as has educational leadership. It is equally as difficult to define leadership as it is to define motivation because of the many view postulated by educational researchers. Owens (1998) describes leadership "as one of the most fascinating topics in organizational behavior and at the same time a notoriously slippery concept that has produced literally hundreds of definitions" (p. 200).

The multiplicity of definitions are highlighted in a survey that reported more than 350 definitions of leadership. Two themes were common among the definitions of leadership, however, (a) "Leadership is a group function: It occurs only in the processes of two or more people interacting. (b) Leaders intentionally seek to influence the behavior of other"(Owens, 1998, p. 200).

Leadership has been described as "not something that one does to people, nor is it a manner of behaving toward people to achieve organizational goals"

(Owens, 1998, p. 206). Barker (1992) contended that "a leader is a person you will follow to a place you wouldn't go by your self' (p. 63). Bennis (1997) explained the difference between a leader and a manager as a means of explaining their definitive roles.

According to Bennis (1997) "more than anything else the difference between a manager rests on the status quo: Managers are willing to live it, leaders are not .. .leaders are the ones with vision, who inspire others to galvanize their efforts and achieve change" (Bennis, 1997, p. 17). "This invariably means that leaders have agendas, they are results oriented. They adopt challenging new visions of what is both possible and desirable, communicate their visions and persuade others to become so committed to these new directions that they are eager to lend their resources and energies to make it happen" (Nanus, 1992, p. 4).

Sergiovanni (1996) found that "Leadership practices based on bureaucratic and personal authority are variations of a strategy that emphasizes follow me. Community theory forces us to understand leadership differently. The emphasis on community leadership is building a shared followership" (p. 83). In this case, leadership tends to be idea - based and it is in this context that principals can sell their vision of what the school can become.

Fullan (2002) explained that leaders have a deeper and more lasting influence on organizations and provide more comprehensive leadership if their performance is not limited to the maintenance of a set of standards. Collins (2001) examined eleven businesses with a minimum of fifteen years of sustained economic performance each.

The study identified the effective leader as the individual who catalyzes commitment to a compelling vision and drives members of the organization to enduring greatness.

The best examples of school system success represent accomplishment at the effective level. That is, they demonstrate high performance standard with corresponding results. When the goal is sustainable change in a knowledge society, business and educational leaders have more in common. Like the business leader, the principal of the future

- the cultural change principal - must be attuned to the big picture, a sophisticated conceptual thinker who transforms the organization through people and teams (Fullan, 2001).

Characteristics of Leadership Defined

The concept of leadership is such a complex phenomena that its characteristics can be defined in different ways. For example, some scholars try to distinguish leaders from authority figures. Leaders relate to followers in ways that:

(1) Motivate them to unite with others in sharing a vision of where the organization should be going and how to get it there.
(2) Arouse their personal commitment to the effort to bring the vision of a better future into being.
(3) Organize the working environment so that the envisioned goals become central values in the organization.
(4) Facilitate the work that followers need to achieve the vision (Owens, 1998, p. 206).

Other scholars (Schwahn & Spady 1998) have defined leadership within five broad dimensions and functions which they call "total leadership." They describe leadership within the following five domains:

(1) Authentic leadership, which embodies purpose, value and meaning through out the organization.
(2) Visionary leadership which is about creating innovative possibilities that shape organizational direction and performance.

(3) Cultural leadership, which is about developing meaning and ownership for innovation and quality through out the organization
(4) Quality leadership is about building continuous improvement capacities and strategies through out the organization.
(5) Service leadership is about supporting empowered workers to accomplish the organizations purpose and vision. (Schwahn & Spady, 1.998, p. 29).

In this analysis, leadership is not seen as a top-down, but rather a collaboration of activities by the individuals which makes for the smooth running of an organization.

Lewin, Lippitt, and White (1939) conducted research that provided new insights into leadership approaches and resulting human behavior. Their studies described leadership as democratic, authoritarian or laissez-faire.

> Democratic leadership is characterized by a structured but Cooperative approach to decision making. It focuses on group relationships and sensitivity to the needs of the people in the organization. Authoritarian leadership is characterized by autocratic methods at arriving **at** decisions with power vested in the upper hierarchy of the organization. Laissez-faire however, is characterized by little structure which provides **for** great latitude **for** personnel worker initiative. (Webb & Norton, 1999 p. 46)

The literature in the area of leadership is very broad because in addition to the scope of its study, the understanding of leadership is undergoing great upheavals in all fields of human endeavor (Owens, 1998). Leadership literature stresses the importance of interaction with others, as leaders impacts and influences the behavior of other people. (Sergiovanni, 1996) argued that all theories of leadership aim at connecting people to each other, and all theories of leadership invariably lead to connecting people to their work.

The various definition of leadership suggest that it is quite a daunting task to articulate one definition type of definition that suit all disciplines. Part of the difficulty lies in the fact that leadership philosophies and processes have evolved over the years, thus, the next section will present a historical overview of leadership.

Historical Overview of Leadership

The literature in the area of leadership features the following:

(1) Scientific Management - (1900's - 1935)
(2) Human Relations -(1935 - 1950's)
(3) Systems Approach - (1950's - 1960's)
(4) Post Modernism - (1970's - 1990's)

"Before the 1930s the few writers and thinkers who concerned themselves with management - beginning with Frederick Winslow Taylor around the tum of the century and ending with Chester Barnard just before World War II- all assumed that business management is **just** a subspecies of general management" (Drucker, 1999, p. 6).

The concept of management as a science grew steadily during the first half of the century, but World War II stimulated its development enormously (Owens, 1998). The scientific management era consisted of a bureaucratic, traditional attitude toward leadership. Great efforts were made to lower costs and lower productivity (Owens, 1995).

The role of the worker was to get the job done in the most efficient manner. The role of the manager is to control, to organize and to give the necessary supervision to ensure that the workers complied with the rules and regulations without unnecessary questioning of management. In fact, the common picture presented of this type of bureaucratic leader is that of the Lone Ranger (Owens, 1998).

Frederick Winslow Taylor (1856 - 1915), the inventor of "Scientific Management," in all probability also coined the terms "management" and "consultant" in their present meaning (Drucker, 1999, p. 6). Taylor's goal was to find solutions to problems throughout industry and factory life. The principles of Scientific Management include: (a) Eliminate guesswork and adopt scientific measure to break the job down to small related tasks, (b) Use scientific methods for selecting and training workers, (c) Establish the clear division of responsibilities between management and workers and establish the discipline whereby management sets the objectives and workers go about achieving them (Callhan, 1962; Owens, 1995). People began to apply the concept of Scientific Management to many aspects of the American life, including the Army, the Navy, the legal profession, education and the household (Callahan, 1962). For example, the first systematic application of scientific management principles was not in business, but rather, "it was in the reorganization of the U.S. Army in 1901 by Elihu Root (1845 - 1937), Theodore Roosevelt's Secretary of War" (Drucker, 1999, p. 7).

The principles of Scientific Management clearly played a significant role in leadership by establishing obvious distinctions between the worker and manager (hierarchical structure). Moreover, it became standard operating procedures for management, hiring and training personnel and provided that the manager was to analyze, plan and control.

Other contributors to the Scientific Management Era and early leadership theory included work by Henri Fayol (1841-1925) who tackled organizational structure as it applied to business in France at the turn of the century. He was head of Europe's largest coal-mining company. Fayol's notable work published in his book *General and Industrial Management,* included defining the "five functions of administration: (a) Planning, (b) Organizing, (c) Commanding, (d) Coordinating, and (e) Controlling" (Owens, 1998, p. 8).

Owens (1998) called attention to the fact that Fayol's use of the words commanding and controlling means leading and evaluating results in the modem era. Fayol later on identified a list of fourteen 'principles' among which were: (a) Unity of command, (b) Authority (c) Initiative, and (d) Moral (Owens, 1998).

During the time of Fayol and Taylor, "It was quite apparent that the Western world was becoming an 'organizational society.' As giant industrial organizations grew in the early 1900's, so did government and other organizational aspects of life grow" (Owens, 1998, p. 9).

The organizational systems that grew in this era did not make life into a utopia. There was a great deal of social, political and economic friction and there were labor unrests and the rise of communism. It was in this setting that the German sociologist, Max Weber "produced some of the most useful, durable, and brilliant work on an administrative system; it seemed promising at the time and has since proved indispensable: bureaucracy" (Owens, 1998 p. 9).

Weber saw hope in bureaucracy because he felt that well - run bureaucracies would become fairer, more impartial and more predictable, than organizations subject to the caprices of powerful individuals. In the ideal bureaucracy,

Weber envisioned certain characteristics that are in a sense, principles of administration:

> A division of labor based on functional specialization.
> A well defined hierarchy of authority.
> A system of rules covering the rights and duties of employees. A system of procedures for dealing with work situations.
> Impersonality of interpersonal relations.
> Selection and promotion based only on technical competence. (Owens, 1998 p. 9)

This era thus recognized the work of three significant people who made great contributions to organizational theories during this period. These three giants of Scientific Management are:

> The American Taylor, who emphasized the principles that viewed administration as management... The Frenchman, Fayol, emphasized broader preparations of administrators so that they would perform their unique functions in the organization more effectively ...
>
> And the German Max Weber, who saw the bureaucratic concept as an attempt to minimize the frustrations and irrationality of large organizations in which the relationships between management and workers are based on class privilege. (Owens, 1998 p. 10)

Human Relations

Mary Parker Follet's work made substantial contributions in the development of management thought. Her ideas were rooted in classical traditions of organizational theory but matured in such a way that she spanned the gap between Scientific Management and the early industrial psychologists. Follet first viewed "management as a social process and second, saw it inextricably enmeshed in the particular situation" (Owens, 1998, p. 13). Follet also stipulated that order is not given by one person but rather all participants should seek to take orders from the situation itself. Follet contended that "the administrator has three choices in the way to handle conflict:

> (a) By the exercise of power (b) By compromise, or (c) By integration" (that is, bringing the conflict in the open and seeking a mutually acceptable win - win resolution) (Owens, 1998 p. 14).

This era is significant for its emphasis on a style of leadership that fosters relationships, interactions, collaboration, and group work. Contemporary thinking about organizational change is greatly influenced by the work of W. Edward Deming's ideas. In fact, Deming's theory of participative management transformed Japanese society during the period of 1950-1980. Deming was also an advocate of empowerment and transforming leadership which he argued were essential to the development of those organizations dedicated to high quality work (Owens, 1998).

The most original of Deming's work included statistical analysis of product quality in mass - production factories. Convinced that power-sharing and unity in the work place were of paramount importance, Deming spent a great deal of time persuading constituents about the merits of participative management.

Social System Theory

Systems theory refutes the notion that phenomena are caused by a single factor. In general, systems can be divided into two main classes: "open" systems which interact with their environment, and "closed" systems which do not interact with their environment. On the whole, social systems theory refers to open systems because it will be difficult to think of an organization such as a school as independent from its environment. However, in the late 1960's and 1970's schools that have resisted interacting with the larger community were often referred to as "closed" systems.

This period reflected the great interest in how organizations function; particularly schools as organizations. This naturally led to an increase of studies about leadership. A number of studies indicated that the leadership styles of this period emphasized structure as well as relationships. Examples of research depicting this trend in leadership include studies at Ohio State, Michigan, and Iowa (Hersey & Blanchard, 1982; Luthuans ,1981). Douglas McGregor's work also emerged at this time. His work is often compared to Rensis Likert who conducted a study of high producing managers (Hersey & Blanchard, 1982). Douglas McGregor developed a theory about leadership based on the leadership assumptions people make about workers. McGregor argued that the transformational leader, unlike the transactional leader, seeks to satisfy the higher needs in the individual and engage the whole person as a follower (Webb & Norton).

This idea converts followers into leaders who can later become moral leaders.

Administrative practices based on management by objectives are based on path goal theory. Raia (1974) contended that in management by objectives "whether or not behavior is satisfying to the individual depends on latent motives and needs"(p. 97). Raia (1974) also viewed MBO's clearly defined work objectives as consistent with path-goal theory of motivation.

Post Modern E:ra

Many scholars have discovered that emerging ideas about reconstructionism during the past two decades, have led to what has been known as the post modem deconstructionist movement (Lopez, 1998). Contemporary post modem theorists have challenged unequal power, and relationships as they apply to class, gender, race and nationalism. In fact, these theorists emphasized importance of democracy while denouncing the politics of exclusion (Webb & Norton, 1999, p. 56).

The application of modem principles have become commonplace in organizations such as business, government and institutions of education. Post modernism is also reflected in the arts, literature, philosophy and architecture (Webb & Norton, 1999).

The major theme shared by many of these post modem theorists is the importance of human resource in any organization. This type of thinking has permeated the workplace and in this modern era, knowledge and skill are integrated at both the operational, strategic, and the transformational levels (Webb & Norton, 1999).

Another major theme during this era is the theme of diversity. Tyson (1995) projected that organization transformation will occur when employees become change agents themselves. Diversity will be depicted in the following ways:

(1) The core will be open - an external market labor market. Although a certain degree of security is

needed, it is more important to ensure a constant flow of ideas.
(2) The core will be diverse. It is vital to obtain a variety of perspectives for innovation to occur: Therefore recruiters will actively seek out people from those already employed.
(3) The culture will be heterogeneous. Instead of having induction and socialization process aimed at homogenizing culture, active steps will be taken to encourage diverse subcultures.
(4) Evaluation of projects will occur during their course and after their completion.

Evaluative criteria will not be limited to the achievement of timetable, budget, and task objectives. Rather, the aim will be to learn from the difficulties experienced and from unexpected outcomes (Webb & Norton, 1999, p. 56).

Other examples of the postmodern movement include Quality of Work Life (QWL), quality circles, Total Quality Management (TQM) and the empowerment of employees through delegation, participation and goal setting (Webb & Norton, 1999).

Contemporary Leadership Theories

In order to understand the various leadership styles of secondary school principals, six contemporary leadership theories will be presented: (a) Theory X, (b) Theory Y, (c) Transformational Leadership, (d) Situational Leadership, (e) Moral Leadership, and (f) Empowerment Leadership.

Theory X and Theory Y set the foundation for many leadership theories that followed. These two theories were early attempts by McGregor (1960) to present a balance between an autocratic and a more democratic perspective of leadership.

Secondly, Situational Leadership is an important example of a leadership theory that examines the balance between concern for task and concern for people. It calls upon the leader to act, using a more directive style of leadership dependent upon the situation.

Transformational leadership is one of the first leadership theories to charge the leader with the major responsibility of being a change agent. Transformational leaders are also viewed as the visionary leaders who "evoke their constituents' better nature and move them toward higher and more universal needs and pmposes" (Bolman & Deal 1997, p. 314). These traits are characteristic of school leaders who embrace school reforms. Common to many leadership theories is the call for leaders to have a vision about the organization's future and motivational skills to move constituents along that path. It is at this juncture that the theory of motivation and various leadership theories unite.

Theory X and Theory Y

In his1960 work, "Douglas McGregor built upon Maslow's theory by adding another central idea: managers' assumptions about workers tend to become self-fulfilling prophecies. and further argued that managers harbor Theory X assumptions - a set of beliefs advocating that subordinates are passive and lazy, have little ambition, prefer to be led and resist change" (Bolman & Deal,1997, p. 105).

McGregor also believed that the lower level needs, physiological and safety, were satisfied by management. Therefore, he contended that more emphasis should be placed on meeting social and self fulfillment needs. Managers who believe in Theory X are likely to see "motivation as basically a matter of the carrot and the stick and they will accept close and detailed supervision of subordinates" (Owens, 1998, p. 36).

TheoryX

Owens (1998) offered four assumptions common to administrators who operate under Theory X: (a) The average person inherently dislikes work and will avoid it whenever possible, (b) Because they dislike work, they must be supervised closely, directed, coerced, or threatened with punishment in order for them put forth adequate effort toward achievement of organization objectives, (c) The average worker will shirk responsibility and seek direction from those in charge and (d) Most workers value job security above other job related factors and have little ambition. According to Owens (1998) administrators who tacitly or explicitly accept assumptions underlying these theories are likely to use them as a guide in dealing with his or her employees.

Ultimately, McGregor concluded that when Theory X assumptions about human nature are universally applied, they are often inaccurate. He further contended that managerial philosophies that emerge from these assumptions may actually fail to motivate many individuals to work toward the organization's goals (Hersey & Blanchard, 1982). McGregor (1960) contended that exhibiting Theory X behaviors was an ineffective motivating strategy since worker's basic needs had already been met and their social, esteem, and self actualizing needs were still emerging. "So long as the assumptions of Theory X continue to influence managerial strategy, we will fail to discover, let alone utilize the potentials of the average human being" (McGregor, 1960, p. 43).

Behavior Associated with Theory X and Theory Y

"The above assumptions about Theory X invariably affect the working relationship between an administrator and an employee. The Theory X administrator is very controlling, directive and acts in a very manipulative way" (Owens, 1998, p. 36). There are two behavior patterns for these managers: One is characterized as "Hard X" on the part of leaders and the other one is known as "Soft X" (Owens, 1998, p. 36).

> Hard X is characterized by no - nonsense, strongly directive Leadership tight controls, and close supervision. Soft X involves a good deal of persuading, "buying" compliance from subordinates, benevolent paternalism, and manipulative human relations. Both behavior patterns are intended to manipulate, control, and manage workers. (Owens, 1998, p. 36)

The question is, in view of the current school reforms and the need to engage educators in teaching and learning, which theory will be most effective for secondary school administrators? Which theory is likely to motivate teachers to move forward with school reforms?

Theory Y

Theory Y proposed that management must provide organizational conditions so that people can achieve their own goals by directing their efforts toward organizational rewards (McGregor, 1960). On the other hand, "if individuals find no satisfaction in their work, then management has no choice but to rely on Theory X to get the work done.

However, the more management aligns organizational requirements with the interests of its employees, the more they can rely on Theory Y for self - direction" (Bolman & Deal, 1997, p. 106).

McGregor's concepts of Theory Y behavior are summarized as follows:

(1) The expenditure of physical and mental effort in work is as natural as play or rest.
(2) External control and threat of punishment are not the only means for bringing about effort toward organizational objectives. People will exercise self-direction and self control in the service of objectives to which they are committed.
(3) Commitment to the objectives is a function of the rewards associated with their achievement.
(4) The average human being learns, under proper conditions, not only to accept but to seek responsibility.
(5) The capacity to exercise a relatively high degree of imagination, ingenuity, and creativity in the solution of organizational problems is widely, not narrowly, distributed in the population.
(6) Under the conditions of modem industrial life, the intellectual potentials of the average human being are only partially realized (Webb & Norton, 1999, p. 51).

McGregor's theory was seen as revolutionary because it emphasized fostering individual self - direction and full potential, exceeding the mere satisfaction of personal needs. McGregor's Theory Y has influenced human resources administration to do the following:

(1) Place new emphasis on the importance of the human dimension in organizations and give a new meaning to the utilization of human resources.

(2) Emphasize the positiveness of employees potential to contribute in intellectual and meaningful ways to organizational effectiveness.
(3) Underline the fallacy of total centralization of administrative actions and emphasize the value of employee participation on a broad scale through out the organization.
(4) Present a new view of expectancy motivation and human behavior in that, when management concepts allow for high-level performance expectations, employee tend to respond (Webb & Norton, 1999, p. 51).

Behavior Associated with Theory Y.

It is quite obvious that the Theory Y manager or school administrator is committed to mutually shared goals and objectives with the worker. The organizational culture led by a manager who fosters trust, communication, respect, work satisfaction and positive interpersonal relationships would be the leader who will motivate people to work harder. There is no doubt that the Theory Y manager "may well be demanding, explicit, and thoroughly realistic, but essentially collaborative" (Owens, 1995, p. 73) Therefore, Theory Y notes that limiting human collaboration in the organizational setting points to managements, limited ingenuity in discovering how to realize the potential represented by its human resources. On the other hand, Theory X management style provides an obvious excuse for ineffective organizational performance (McGregor, 1960).

In conclusion, McGregor's Theories X and Y have shaped managers' and administrators' styles and how they perceive their employees (Heresey & Blanchard, 1993; McGregor, 1960; Owens, 1995).

Transformational Leadership

As proposed by McGregor, Theory Y supports the premise that leadership is dynamic and process oriented. We can see a symbiotic relationship between theory and transformational leadership.

> It is not enough for leaders just to make the right moves for any purpose that suits them, or for any vision that they might have of what schools should be like. The noted historian and leadership theorist, James MacGregor Bums (1978), pointed out that purposes and visions should be socially useful, should serve the common good, should meet the needs of the followers, and should elevate followers to a higher moral level. He calls this kind of leadership transformational. (Sergiovanni, 1996, p. 94)

Therefore, transformational leadership seems to proport the idea of change for the better, for the individual. Invariably, the transformational leader looks for potential motives in followers, seeks to satisfy higher needs, and engages the full person as the follower. The result of transforming leadership is a relationship of mutual stimulation and elevation that converts followers into leaders and may convert leaders into moral agents (Owens, 1998).

An analysis of Bums's theory of the transformational leader lies in sharp contrast with the traditional definition of "transactional" leadership. Bums (1978) explained that leadership is more than just wielding power over people. He further identified two basic types of leadership. In the most common type of leadership style, the relationship between the leader and the followers is based on quid pro quo transactions.

Transactional educational leaders can and do offer protection and the security that employees need and they in turn expect their subordinates to be in compliance to them.

The second type of leadership that is evoked, is the transformational leader. As cited earlier, this type of leadership "looks for potential and motives in followers and looks to satisfy that need and in the process of doing that it changes the climate of the organization, since followers could become leaders" (Owens, 1998). Unequivocally, transformational leaders as the name suggests are change agents and they are always concerned with ways that new ideas and initiatives can be pushed forward within the school system.

The Transformational Leader

The transformational leader is interested in life - long learning. Through purposeful learning situations, the organization is being shaped to meet the needs of the stakeholders. The various participants at all levels are engaged in continuous learning in order to expand their ideas and knowledge about problems that face the organization.

Understandably, the transformational leader is a teacher, a coach, a facilitator and a mentor for their organization (Barth, 1991; Depree, 1987; Senge, 1990; Sergiovanni, 1996).

Secondly, the transformational leader is a leader who is involved in continuous change in order to bring the organization to its highest goal. Thody (1997) states that "it is the transformers amongst English CEOs who are remembered, whose achievements became the expectations for all their successors and who were early expected to play a role in long - term planning" (Thody, 1997, p. 71).

Moral Leadership

It is quite clear that one of the characteristics of a transformational leader is the individual leader's ability to be a change agent. This invariably leads us to a discussion about moral leadership in education. Leadership in a knowledge society can be found around five essential components: (a) Moral purpose, (b) An understanding of the change process, (c) The ability to improve relationships, (d) Knowledge creation, and (e) Sharing and coherence making (Fullan, 2002).

According to Fullan (2002), moral purpose is social responsibility to others and the environment. One of the characteristics of a school leader with a moral purpose is to seek to make a difference in the lives of students. More than anything else, moral leaders in education are also concerned with closing the gap between high - performing and lower - performing students. In order to achieve these goals, they start with making a difference at their schools as well as improving the school community as a whole. These leaders act with intention of making a positive difference in their own schools as well as improving the surrounding areas around the school district (Fullan, 2002).

In order to achieve these objectives, moral leaders maintain strong communication, trust, service to others, recognition to human diversity, empowerment, leading by example, development, sense of community, purpose and principles. A moral leadership's uniqueness lies in the fact it calls for nesting oneself in purpose and moral obligation and commitment to doing the right thing (Sergiovanni, 1992).

Moral leadership can therefore, be viewed as a form of calling in a vocation.

Gardner (1989) contended that" the goal is not an indiscriminate cultivation of all human capacities, but individual fulfillment within a moral framework" (Gardner, 1989, p. 43).

In his paper, *Moral Aspects of Leadership,* Gardner described three attributes of a moral leader, (a) High expectation, (b) Respect for excellence, and (c) Belief in human potential (Gardner, 1989).

Therefore, moral leadership is at the heart of effective leadership. Moral leaders intentionally create a value base. They also maintain very strong communication lines in order to make sure that organizational members are involved in the same dialogue and hence, they are aware of important issues affecting the organization.

Empowered Leadership

Improving the quality of education in a school takes the cooperation of all staff members. Regardless of the ability of a few, the joint efforts of all members are required to bring about positive change. "School principals who tend to operate in a top - down fashion may believe they have control, but they pay for their oppressiveness later on" (Sybouts & Wendel, 1994, p. 162).

This concept of power being maintained by a few, is indicative of the scientific era. This was an era when lower level employees felt powerless because they had no ownership in what went on at their places of employment. However, it is clear that workers are more effective when they have input in the projects ensuing at their work places. Kouzes and Posner (1987) offered corroborating evidence which demonstrates that shared power results in higher job satisfaction.

Moreover, according to Bennis and Townsend (1995) "when a leader creates an atmosphere in which employees feel free to offer contrary views and speak the truth, an empowered workforce is created. Given the power to do what they do best, these motivated individuals serve as vital allies in transforming the organization" (p. 73).

Empowerment has been defined as "a process whereby participants develop the competence to take care of their own growth and resolve their own problems.

Empowered individuals believe they have the skills and knowledge to act on a situation and improve it" (Short & Greer, 1997, p. 134).

Conditions for Empowerment

Empowerment thrives under certain conditions because if that climate is not created, then the individuals do not feel the need to push for goals that will benefit either the individual or the organization. Covey (1992) presented five factors that are necessary for enhancing a culture where empowerment will permeate. These factors are (a) "Evaluate personnel and organizational effectiveness, (b) Focus on creating change, (c) Create win-win agreements (d) Create supportive structures and systems, and (e) Teach, exemplify and reinforce" (Covey, 1992, p. 216).

On the whole, the literature shows that in order for empowerment to thrive, it must be part of the organizational goals which becomes part of the culture of the school. Short and Greer (1997) presented similar cultural conditions necessary for empowerment to exist (a) "Clear directions from management that identify the organizational goals without specifying the means, (b) Performance - unit structures must be developed that are enabling, (c) Organizational context must be supportive by providing a non-divisive reward structure, an education and information system, (d) Coaching and consultation, and (e) Teams must have adequate material resources" (Short & Greer, 1997, p. 132).

When the above conditions exist, then individuals feel empowered and that leads to productivity and effectiveness. This is because "effective administrators make sure that someone is attending to all important areas of school life - themselves or others"

(Sybouts & Wendell, 1994, p. 162). The fact that the school leader empowers others does not leave him or her powerless, but rather it is the mindset that allows the leader to join forces with followers to work toward a common goal.

Empowered leadership calls for leader and followers to work together. In order to understand empowerment, it can be contrasted with the autocratic style of leadership, where power was enjoyed by an individual or by few people. Empowered leadership is a process of empowering people so that they can realize and use their untapped potential.

Effective leader recognize individuals with potential in certain areas. It then becomes the leader's job to empower these individuals through motivation, to bring out their best.

New Roles for Secondary School Principals

As noted in the conceptual framework, **a** principal' s performance is a conglomeration of several interacting factors. Although there have been several studies published about the different aspects of **the** performance of the successful secondary school principal, there are limited number of studies focusing on the totality of factors that made these principals successful.

However, there are numerous studies which cite the principal as the precursor to a successful school. For example, Johnson (1993) conducted a study to establish a relationship between organizational effectiveness and the effectiveness of organizational leaders. The sample for this study was drawn from 112 elementary school principals in Alberta Canada.

The results of this study, according to Johnson (1993), support a close relationship between the two constructs and highlight the complexity of educational leadership.

The educational literature offer a number of studies citing the school principal as the most important catalyst in any successful school (Bookbinder, 1992). "Leadership has been viewed much more of an art, a belief, a condition of the heart, than a set of things to do. The visible signs of artful leadership are expressed ultimately in its practice" (De Pree, 1989, p. 11). If it is in fact true that the principal is the most important person in a school setting, what characteristics should he or she display in order for him to be seen as successful?

Historical Overview of the Principalship

The role of the principal emerged as a result of an increasing population between the 1850's - 1900's which meant that schools were going to be needed for children. "The headmaster in early American schools was appointed when the number of students and teachers became so large that boards of directors or elders in the church saw a need for management and control over staff and students" (Sybouts & Wendel, 1994). The initial role of the principals was mainly clerical, and they were often called Headmasters or Head Teachers. It was around the 1800's that the role shifted to that of supervision and management. "By the early 1900's, three critical and enduring functions of the principalship had gained a secure footing: (a) The general organization and management of the school, (b) The supervision of instruction and staff development, and (c) The interpretation of the work of the school to the immediate school community" (Bookbinder, 1992, p. 11).

The term "principal" was derived from prince and it means first in rank, degree or importance, and authority. The principal, therefore, was the person with authority to make decisions about the operations of the school. According to most accounts, the formal designation of a principal was in Cincinnati about the middle of the 19th century, yet the position of a school principal is a 2ot11 cen tury development (Kimbrough & Burkett, 1990).

In fact, some of the pivotal changes in the principalship include the range of expectations placed on the position; these expectations have moved from demands for management and control, with presumptions for forced compliance, to the demand for an educational leader who can foster staff development, program improvement, parent involvement, community support and student growth (Sybouts & Wendel, 1994).

The Current State of the Prindpalship

As a result of the national shortage of secondary school principals, researchers are beginning to study the new roles for the secondary school principal. In examining the state of the principalship, researchers have identified factors that have added to the overload. These include the new roles placed on secondary school principals. The descriptions of the new roles of principals continue to evolve in response to the changes and demands of society. Fullan (1998) succinctly defined the new role of the principals:

> Wanted: A miracle worker who can do more with less, Pacify rival groups, endure chronic second - guessing, tolerate low levels of support, process large volumes of paper and work double shifts (75 nights a year out). He

or she will have carte blanche to innovate, but cannot spend much money, replace any personnel or upset any constituency. (Evans, 1995, p. 29-36)

The State of the Prindpalship

The literature about the school principalship has emphasized the stresses of the principal's work (Whitaker, 1994). Studies have described the principalship as filled with conflict, unsatisfying management requirements, with long days and nights (Duke

1988; Gmelch & Chan 1994). Attrition has increased and candidates pools have shrunk, and pundits have blamed it on these unsatisfactory conditions (Donaldson, 1999).

Studies reveal that there is cause for concern for the principalship (ERS 1988, p. 25). Clearly, "these are indeed tough times for many secondary school principals and some of them have come to question what their schools stand for. Many of the school principals experience an erosion in commitment and in one way or the other are giving up" (Fullan, 1997, p. vii).

According to Checkley (2000), the search is on across the United States. For example, from Old Saybrook, Connecticut, to Salinas, California, from Patch Grove, Wisconsin, to Plano, Texas, schools across the United States are looking for strong leaders. The major problem with this search is that there may not be enough strong leaders to go around. In addition, superintendents reported difficulty in finding principals who are capable of providing effective leadership. One reason for this, some superintendents suggested, is **that** the definition of "effective leadership" has changed significantly and the contemporary principal has to manage far more administrative tasks than traditionally associated with running a school (Checkley, 2000).

This state of affairs accounts for the increasing nation - wide shortage of principals. Whaley (2002) affirms that a report released on Wednesday, January 23, 2002 in Colorado stated that 740 principal positions will be open in the state's 176 school districts over the next five years, and there is no clear direction as to how those vacancies are going to be filled. This type of situation gives concerned citizens a clear example of the extent of the shortage in some states.

This problem is exacerbated by the fact that principals are caught within two worlds; internal and external worlds. Principals receive limited support as leaders or managers within their school setting because of the tremendous demands being made on them by teachers, parents and students (Sybouts & Wendel, 1994).

What principals do to get through each day seems to be far removed from the visions of dynamic inspirational leadership to which they once aspired. As a result of the multiplicity of tasks they have to perform, and the different political groups that seem to infringe on their power, sometimes school leaders do not feel they have any meaningful power (Lashway, 1998). There is no doubt that one of the reasons secondary school principals are leaving the job is because of "overload." (Fullan (1998), reported findings from a study presented to the Toronto Board of Education that suggested a relationship between the roles of principals and the ever - increasing expectations placed on them.

The sample included made up of 137 principals and vice - principals on the Toronto Board of Education who were asked to rate eleven major expectations of the job. The results of the study showed that on the average, across all eleven dimensions, 90% of the principals and vice principals reported an increase in demands, with only 9% citing a decrease. Almost all the principals in this study, mentioned a specific addition to their work load ranging from new initiatives, curriculum and multicultural issues. The overload stems from the fact that most of these principals have to continue to operate as their building managers as well as carrying out new initiatives and reforms. Yerkes and Guaglianone (1998) explained that a review of the literature showed that principal worked approximately 60-80 hours a week and there is minimal pay differential between the top teacher and the administrator.

As building managers, they are constantly bombarded with interruptions on the job which has very little to do with school reform or the type of leadership they envisioned as aspiring principals (Fullan, 1997). That study echoed the concerns of Murphy and Beck, (1994), who write that principals occupy a role with contradictory demands. The contradiction is around the fact that as middle managers, principals have to maintain rapport with teachers as well as well as those in the hierarchy. In addition to that, Principals are asked to push forward reform agendas they have no hand in developing. Principals are also expected to be actively involved in the transformation, restructuring and redefinition of schools while they maintain their organizational positions as managers which sometimes resists change.

It is clear that the factors that have added to the overload of the secondary school principal are the different roles they have to take on at their various schools and at the same time assert influence on the voluntary behavior of others in their building, in order to draw them together for cooperative efforts (Strodl, 1993) As cited earlier, another definitive role for the school principal, is the paradigm shift from being a building manager to that of an instructional leader in order to facilitate teaching and learning.

The Principal as Instructional Leader

The current expectation placed on most secondary school principals, is that they act as instructional leaders at their particular schools. Dufour (2002) stated that schools need leadership from principals who focus on students' learning as well as teaching. The principal must serve as an instructional leader of the school. For more than 30 years, research has described the principal in this way, and the National Association of

Secondary School Principals (2001) corroborated by defining its mission, in part, as strengthening the role of the principal as instructional leader.

This means that the principal will be held responsible for driving new curriculum and other initiatives that involve teaching and learning as well as being managers of their building. Perkins-Gough (2002) found that instructional leadership is intertwined with educational leadership and the two cannot be separated. Good educational leaders keep student learning at the focal point of their administration. As instructional leaders, some scholars are advocating that the principal's focus be driven by the following personal questions: "To what extent are the students learning the intended outcomes of each course? What steps can I take to give both students and teachers the additional time and support they need to improve learning" (DuFour, 2002 p. 13).

This emphasis and shift from teaching to learning is not mere semantics. It is undoubtedly clear the principal and all constituents are focused on learning the culture of the school begins to change in substantive ways. Principals foster this structural and cultural transformation when they shift their emphasis from helping individual teachers improve instruction to helping teams of teachers ensure that students achieve the intended outcomes of their schooling (DuFour, 2002).

In order to become an effective instructional leader, it sometimes means changing the climate of the school - which may be toxic. It may be that the most difficult job of an instructional leader is to change the prevailing culture of the school. The culture of a school dictates in no uncertain terms, "the way we do things around here." A leader cannot change the culture of a school alone, however, "one can provide forms of leadership that invite others to join as observers of the old and architects of the new" (Barth, 2002, p. 6).

It has been suggested "that effective principals make choices as instructional leaders to engage in activities that directly affect teachers, classrooms, curricula, and students" (Hart & Bredson, 1996, p. 213). Moreover, another positive contribution is for principals to have direct influence on instruction through professional development activities, modeling coaching and teaching (Hart & Bredson, 1996). Smith and Andrews (1989) stated that as an instructional leader, the principal is perceived as providing the needed support and resources for teachers to teach and for students to learn. They should also have a complete understanding of the curriculum and best practices, and they should be a good listener and communicator.

Behavior, practices and specific indicators of principals as instructional leaders include the following:

(1) Commitment to and articulation of high expectations for staff
(2) Development of clear vision and goals focused on enhancement of student achievement
(3) Understanding of curriculum and instruction
(4) Implementation of district curriculum
(5) Monitoring of student academic progress

(6) Provision of resources to support curriculum and instruction
(7) Implementation of professional development
(8) Assurance of ample classroom time for instruction; and understanding of adult learning (Bookbinder, 1992; Hart & Bredson, 1996; Lipham, 1981; Richardson,

et al.,1983; Smith & Andrews,1989; Sybouts & Wendel, 1994).

In all, the principal is required to play the important role of initiating, facilitating and sustaining the process of shifting our collective focus from teaching to learning. This will be possible, if teachers are given the opportunity to collaborate in teams so that they can become the primary engine of school improvement (DuFour, 2002).

As cited in this study, the secondary school principal faces constant demands that interfere with their ability to perform as instructional leaders and at the same time as managers (Fullan, 1997; Smith & Andrews, 1989). Principals are confronted with daily issues related to management, student discipline, employee relations, and parent and community development. Since more demands are being placed on principals, scholars are wondering how they can fulfill these responsibilities while concurrently assuming effective roles as instructional leaders.

Although educators are advocating change in the role of the secondary school principal, it still stands to reason that the effective running of a school requires a manager who can recognize problems quickly and take decisive action (Bowen, Lewicki, Hall & Hall, 1997). Secondary school principals are responsible for managing budget, facilities, curricular and extra curricular activities, social services, human and other resources, and programs. "The skill of the principal, while performing as the school manager, is a vital factor in the school's ability to respond to its internal and external environmental tasks and challenges" (Bookbinder, 1992, p. 59). This significant role of the principal as a manager leads to the debate on the role of the school principal as an instructional leader versus a manager. Neil (1993) conducted a study entitled *The Principal and School Effectiveness: Principals Perspectives.* The sample included 112 elementary school principals in Alberta (Canada) who rated effectiveness on 38 organizational and 29 leadership criteria. Results support a close relationship between the two constructs and highlight the complexity of educational leadership.

The literature emphasizes the school leader as an instructional leader. However, Bookbinder (1992, p. 17) stated that "high performing organizations have both order and meaning, structure and values. They accomplish goals while attending to core values and beliefs. They encourage both leadership and management, symbolic behavior and technical activity" (Deal & Peterson, 1994, p. 9).

Lipham (1981, p. 7) stated that "effective principals recognize and accept the fact that a substantial amount of their time and energy must be expanded in dealing with internal school issues and concerns." This shows that the two concepts are inextricably linked together and it may take real skill on the part of the school principal to perform both tasks effectively. This means that although principals need to fulfill their roles as managers to bring order and stability to the school, their role as instructional leaders takes precedence over their managerial tasks. This is because their role as an instructional leader aligns with the ideas of current educational reform, which is why they are currently being held accountable for student achievement.

The Principal's Influence on Student Achievement

Erickson (1998) argued that in school "in school districts across the United States, the tension to meet academic standards is because the stakes are high. General views of education are fueled by the publication of test scores in local newspapers" (p. vii). This practice has become the norm because in as much as many American educators say that a student's performance should not be judged by the results of one standardized test score, it continues to be the practice, and educators are held accountable for these results.

The emphasis on test results became widespread after the publication of the *A Nation at Risk: The Imperative for Educational Reform* (1983). This publication revealed the low academic performance of some of our public schools students and through out the country educators were looking for reliable methods for raising academic standards. In this article, The National Commission on Excellence in Education charged that the American people have:

> in effect been committing an act of unilateral education disarmament. Our society and its educational institutions seem to have lost sight of the basic purposes of schooling, and the high expectations and disciplined effort needed to attain them. (p. 2)

The academic performance of some of America's public school students lends support to the Commissioner's statement. Therefore, researchers seek to identify the factors that make other secondary principals successful in the face of such difficulties and expectations. Erickson (1998) concluded that "when the United States had an economy that operated to a large extent within its boarders and was based on local industry and national corporations, the concern over education was not so pronounced" (p. 1). It is unequivocally clear that the role of the principal has been under great scrutiny.

As previously cited, secondary school principals are expected to assume the role of instructional leaders, and it is therefore not surprising that for the most part, they are held accountable for the achievement of their students.

As a result of the new expectations placed on school principals, Ewing (2001) conducted a study on accountable leadership to determine if there was a relationship between the leadership style of a principal and student achievement. The study surveyed 50 principals and 750 teachers from high - middle - and low-achieving elementary schools public schools in Chicago. Leadership styles were identified according to Blanchard's Model of Situational Leadership II.

The findings indicated that situational leadership styles of the principal were significantly related to student achievement in reading and mathematics. The study indicated that the more increased use of high flexibility (equal use of style selection) practiced by the principal, the more there was increased use of successful effectiveness (that is, the most appropriate style selection for the situation).

It is therefore quite obvious that in schools where achievement was high, invariably, the principal made the difference (Boyer, 1985). Studies on effective schools reflect the view that the direct responsibility for improving instruction and learning rests in the hands of the school principal (Smith & Andrews, 1989). Hart and Bredson (1996) postulated that the improvement of learning outcomes is the clearest and least contestable of goals stated for reform across the nation. Principals are clearly held accountable for increase in student achievement in all areas because they have to ensure that the right curriculum and resources are in place for students.

If principals are held accountable for their students' achievement, then it invariably means that they will be held accountable for the performance of their students on the various standardized tests and consequently, the results of these tests became part of their evaluation. To that end, (Verona, 2001) conducted a study on" *The Influence of Principal Transformational Leadership Style on High School Proficiency Test results in New Jersey's Comprehensive and Vocational - Technical High Schools.*

This study used Leithwood's Model of Transformational Leadership, which adapts Bass and Avolio's Transformational and Transactional Leadership Theory to schools, to conceptualize principal leadership. The main result of this study is that transformational leadership by principals significantly affects the High School Proficiency Test (HSPT) passing rates in reading, mathematics, writing, and all sections combined on the HSPT. Additionally, the results show that to achieve the same HSPT passing rates, stronger transformational leadership is needed in vocational schools than in comprehensive high schools (Verona, 2000).

Skills Inherent to Successful Principals

The previous section elicited the roles of the effective principals and the evolution that led to that stage. Since professional jobs require mastery of certain core ideas and processes, the skills necessary for effective principals to fulfill their roles will be discussed in this section. The principal's role has been identified as the single most important factor in determining a school's effectiveness and there are specific behavior characteristics related to leadership (NAESP, 1991). While it seemed unrealistic to expect principals to possess all the identified characteristics, however, proficiencies could become goals that effective elementary and middle school principals could be aim to achieve.

A review of the literature presented be NAESP (1991) indicated skills that are essential for proficiency in the principalship. The first three are a direct function of educational preparation:

(1) Advanced skills in the teaching and learning processes
(2) A thorough understanding of practical applications of child growth and development
(3) A solid background in the liberal arts
(4) The fourth prerequisite and the most important, consists of sincere commitment to children's welfare and progress (NAEP, 1991, p. 3).

Another skill which the elementary or secondary school principal must possess is that 'they must be leaders of leaders' hence, these are leaders who tend to share and they have a determination to always improve. As a result of that they see themselves as educational leaders and they are involved in constructive changes within their schools (NAESP, 1991).

A review of the literature indicates that principals need to possess the following skills: Lopez (1998).

(1) The ability to promote harmony within the school setting and achieving a sense of common purpose
(2) Good communication- the image such principals project, both verbally and non verbally and in written communication forms the dominant perception of the school on the part of students, staff, parents and the community
(3) High motivation

(4) Has the skill to create a caring community in which every student can experience success
(5) futerpersonal relationships
(6) fuitiative - for example, this leader spells out what students are to learn and what teachers are to teach
(7) Enthusiasm-these principals are concerned that students and staff alike achieve their potential
(8) Self confidence
(9) Organization and follow through
(10) The effective principal must know how to handle political pressures
(11) Decision making
(12) Technical (law, budget, finance, technology). The effective principal must have a proficiency in managing the school's organization and its fiscal resources. (Depree, 1987; Hart & Bredson, 1996; Richardson, et al., 1993; NAESP, 1991, Sybouts & Wendel, 1994).

The National Association of Secondary School Principals (1975) has designed an assessment to evaluate principal's skills related to job performance. The twelve skills are: (a) Problem analysis, (b) Judgment, (c) Organizational ability, (d) Decisiveness, (e) Leadership, (f) Sensitivity, (g) Stress tolerance, (h) Oral communication, (i) Written communication, (j) Range of interest, (k) Personal motivation, and (l) Educational values (Lipham, 1981; Sybouts & Wendel, 1994). The first four skills; problem analysis, judgment, organizational ability, and decisiveness fall within administrative tasks performed by the secondary school principal. The other skills are categorized as interpersonal skills, communication skills and values, which if used well can motivate teachers and other staff members.

Research suggested that the skills needed to be an effective secondary school principal are vast. Around leadership behavior, the individual must be able to analyze relevant information, make decisions, delegate responsibility and provide appropriate support and follow - up (NAESP, 1991). The effective secondary school principal must be able to advance the profession through the participation as a member of local and national professional groups.

The principal must have good interpersonal skills both internal and external communities. The human relations skills include the ability to supervise individuals, support people in growth and development; and build on human diversity.

Development of Principals

The demands of the principalship have multiplied, even as they shared their authority with school improvement teams. "The public is demanding more explicit evidence that educational programs are achieving the desired impacts. In addition, federal and state legislative guidelines are placing demands on the principal's time, making the job even more demanding" (Barth, 1990, p. 65).

"To be able to take care, provide for the safety and educate hundreds of other people's children ten months of the year will require an individual with extraordinary skills and qualities, and that is where principal preparation and development comes in to place" (Barth, 1990, p. 65). It is along these lines that the phases of principal development, principal preparation, principal induction, and development for experienced principals were explored. Local universities, state departments and businesses are collaborating with school districts to develop both new and experienced principals.

In fact, many states across the nation are requiring training and development as part of the certification renewal. In all the phases of principal development there exist components which include mentoring, establishing support systems, formal training, and other kinds of development.

As cited earlier, various constituencies including stakeholders parents state and federal agencies have placed tremendous demands on the school principal to make the school more effective. This has led to major school reforms across the nation. Moreover, the secondary school principal is constantly being bombarded with various demands that makes their job very challenging. Barth (1990) postulated that lack of specific knowledge and skills needed by principals in order for them be effective seem to be the immediate problem at a time when huge demands are being placed on them.

> Ironically, it is obvious that the absolute authority once Enjoyed by the principal is now being shared with school Improvement teams, which comprises of teachers, students and parents, who put tremendous pressure on the principal. The stress that principals face has been compounded by a large number of problems. The principal' s job which was once stable, faces significant attrition every year. (Barth,1990, p. 65)

Research suggests that sometimes principals who are deemed as "successful" are the very people who leave the profession. The reasons for leaving indicated by these individuals, include the heavy demands placed on them by the principalship. Some of these unfavorable conditions for the principals was noted by Barth (1990) in an informal survey of principals and the results are the following:

Excessive time demands	56%
Stress (emotional health)	52%
Desire for change	40%
Heavy work load	51%
Fatigue	37%
Lack of support from superiors	35%
Courts/legislation	35%
Lack of teacher professionalism	35%
Student Discipline	29%
Student apathy	28% (Barth, 1990, p. 65).

It is clear that the number of educators assuming the principalship is depleting, and that will ultimately affect teachers, students and the rest of the community. In order for principals to be effective and to have the desired influence on the professional development of teachers and the achievement of students, training and development processes must be altered. "The principal required to effectively and productively orchestrate and lead the restructuring, renewal reforms will need to be a new breed of administrator. His or her preparation and professional development programs must focus on the areas of content knowledge, skills and leadership ability required of those who are to make a difference in the school" (Bookbinder, 1992, p. 29).

Phases of Principal Development

Principal Preparation

According to Barth (1990), research seeking to determine what contributed most to principals' success generally finds that, academic preparation ranked at the bottom of the list. These findings suggest the need for pre - service programs for principals. As a result of the problems inherent to principalship, certificate programs are being restructured.

In the past, an individual interested in the school principalship taught for several years and then began a program of studies at a local college (Daresh, 1990). In fact, sometimes an individual became a principal not because he or she possessed qualities of leadership, but rather, because they had climbed the ladder to a better paying job. Again, sometimes in the past, individuals have been selected because oftheir abilities to "manage," which naturally and stereotypically made school administrators a male dominated job.

Keller (2000), an independent education researcher and writer, recalled visiting principals' preparation program a decade ago, and noted for the most part that the courses were textbook based and the classes were boring. In addition Keller (2000) asserted that there was no screening of aspiring principals and most of the time the students were on their own.

In order to ascertain whether there is need to improve the way principals are prepared, Johnson and Snyder (1990), developed a research instrument to assess the perceived training needs of school administrators. A pilot study of 442 administrators identified principalship, problem solving and staff development as their areas of greatest concern.

To be able to solve some of the problems associated with principal preparation program, some have become more comprehensive. State departments of education, universities, and school systems have become partners with some states in planning and implementing preparation and development programs for principals. Licata, Joseph, Elliot and Chad (1990), found that there is a movement through the United States to provide a network of support and information for leadership in educational administration and for new principals. Stakeholders and policy makers are beginning to respond to the need for updated, comprehensive professional development.

Alternate Preparation Programs for Principals

In an effort to identify preparation programs that align with the rigorous demands placed on principals, Schmuck (1993) conducted a study of a two year experimental program in Oregon designed for administrators. The participants (aspiring principals) in this study spent seven weekends at the institute where they focused on administrative skills and contemporary instructional leadership. During the following summer, the participants took four management courses and participated in the National Association of Secondary School Principals (NASSP) Assessment Center; a field based mentoring experience. Schmuck's (1993) study revealed the following:

   (1) Most participants were capable of articulating a coherent philosophy and applied skills during their mentorship.
   (2) Participants had favorable attitudes toward their training program and a deeper understanding of

leadership than their counterparts in the traditional program.
(3) Experimental participants were much more successful in procuring administrative positions than their counterparts.
(4) Most participants negotiated their first year successfully.

Corroborating evidence was offered by Erlandson and Zellner (1997), who explained that the Principals' Center at Texas A & M University established a school leadership initiative (SLI). The initiative focused on the 21 principal domains previously identified by the National Policy for Educational Administration. The participants in this program attended retreats and monthly seminars examined their leadership skills, and met regularly throughout the year. In addition, they also communicated by electronic mail, video conferencing, on - site visits and through reflective journals.

Summative data gathered from the program's first year points to the importance of including training opportunities, such as effective mentoring for personal professional growth and campus leadership development (Erlandson, & Zellner, 1997).

The purpose of these kinds of alternate programs, is to help the novice principals to establish a pattern of continuous learning, growth and professional development (Daresh & Playko, 1992).

Mentoring

"Mentoring is the process of transforming a novice into an expert by helping that individual acquire skills, attitudes and knowledge in a chosen field" (Parks, 1991, p. 8). Therefore, in an attempt to find new ways of training prospective principals Crow and Matthews (1998), stated that since the huge school reforms going on can place educators in 'unchartered territory,' it is very important that school principals get involved in a career - long mentoring approach. This approach will help principals to stay abreast of new reform ideas that sweep across the various districts.

Crow and Matthews (1998) advocated for a process that describes mentoring as a socialization process, which lays emphasis on the characteristics that one would look for in a school principal. Their study also revealed the importance of organization, planning, selection, matching and evaluation in a mentoring program, which can lead to successful leadership.

Daresh and Playko, (1992), also conducted a study and found that structured and formal mentoring activities are appropriate and useful for novice principals. This research also supports the practice of authentic of professional development for principals who are currently serving in the system so as to develop their skills to respond to contemporary times.

With reference to mentoring as a form of preparation for aspiring principals, Mann (1998), stipulated that school principals and assistant principals would be well served by meaningful professional development. This additional professional development is important because while some research suggests that some people are born with leadership skills, it is clear also from the literature that leadership abilities can be cultivated and nurtured. Mann (1998) further argued that leadership can be fostered through coaching, mentoring, networking and study groups.

Mann (1998) supported these kinds of development activities, noting that in - service has historically been lacking in relevance and impact because it is often after thought.

Therefore, the challenge will be to adopt new approaches to professional development that draw on current research.

On the whole, the alternative that researchers are calling for to improve the preparation of principals, is one that requires individuals to engage in reflective practice (Wise, 1992). To that end Wise (1992) conducted a study that examined the relationship between theory and real - life conditions in the preparatory program. Of particular benefit to the participants were seminars, internships, mentorship, reflective practices and cohort groups. These activities afforded participants the opportunity to personalize their ideas so that by the end of the program, they would have developed reflective, responsive skills.

Training and Development of Experienced Principals

Barth (1990) argued that "if the work that principals do is to be thoughtful and rigorous, then so should the certification requirements and the formal academic course work preparing principals for the profession" (Barth, 1990, p. 66). Sergiovanni (1996) contended that school leaders will have to go through a selection and training process in order for them to fit the requirements of the new era. In addition to modification in certification requirements,

> what the principal needs most is support and assistance. This is because, every principal, novice and veteran alike are in and out of 'hot water' all the time, and these moment of conflict provide great potential for learning. What the principal needs at this time is helpful nonjudgemental assistance reflecting and sharpening professional practice. (Barth, 1990, p. 68)

Another model for principal development used in a large school system in Florida, assigns a three member support team to the principal. The support team, together with the principal, design an individualized professional development plan. Members of the support team serve as mentors, coaches, advisors, and monitor the individual progress (Morsie, 1990).

The principal is the most important person in the school in terms of school's effectiveness. Yet, there has been a national cry to refine principal preparation programs partly because of the high attrition rates among principals.

Historically, training and development of experienced principals was not a common practice. However, researchers and other stakeholders now recognize the importance of including principals in the continuous learning process. In fact, Barth, (1990) argued that "as learners principals have a bad reputation" (p. 68). This is often due to the perception that a principal's time is spent on other issues other than their own professional development.

Currently, however, escalating attrition as a result of the attrition rates among the principalship, the training and development of experienced principals has become an issue of priority within various school districts. Components of these programs usually include establishing support systems internally as well as externally, mentoring, opportunities for reflection, and establishing personal platforms.

> Finally, if principals do engage in the learning experience and learn something - a new way of thinking about the curriculum, a new interpersonal skill, a new about improving school climate - they are often faced with having to do something with it. (Barth, 1990, p. 70)

Thus, although it is good practice to be involved in continuous training, some principals tend to fear the additional work it might add to their already busy schedule.

Summary

Chapter Two featured a review of the literature about Motivation, Leadership, Successful Principals, and Development of Principals. These particular phenomena were selected as a basis to support the problem for this study - factors that contribute to successful principals: The Rhode Island Experience.

Research about motivation examined why individuals are motivated to succeed and achieve. Findings from a number of studies conducted during the mid - part of the 20th century revealed that individuals in work place settings are motivated by being engaged in group processes and decision making, having opportunities for growth development, achieve self - actualization by having control over their work, assuming responsibility, and receiving recognition.

Various theories of leadership were explored and a relationship was identified between the leadership theories and the early theories of motivation. The research revealed that leadership theories such as the transformational theory, moral theory and empowerment are based on the notion that the leader and the follower develop and self - actualize. These leadership theories align closely with Maslow's Hierarchy and Herzberg's Two Factor Model, which focus on higher levels of esteem, self-actualization and content satisfiers (achievement, recognition, responsibility, work itself, and advancement).

Next, research about successful principals was reviewed for three reasons. First, it is closely linked with the research on leadership in that an effective principal must be a leader who collaborates and also develops leadership qualities in others. Secondly, the literature about successful principals indicates that the ability to motivate teachers and students to engage in meaningful reforms will lead to achievement. Finally, the body of literature also focused on specific skills that principals need in order for them to be successful.

The literature also revealed that authentic, appropriate, and timely professional development of principals is a national priority. Engaging principals in continuous learning, through mentoring, reflection, support systems and other means will contribute to their success in a particularly critical and difficult role.

Chapter three will present the methodology utilized in the study.

CHAPTER THREE

METHODOLOGY

This exploratory study investigated the factors that contribute to successful principals, and was based on a sample of principals from the state of Rhode Island. Chapter Three, the Methodology, was designed to include the Statement of the Problem, Research Design and Methodology, Populations and Sample Identification, Instrumentation, Data Collection Procedures, as well as Data Analysis.

Statement of the Problem

Since successful schools seem to be dependent on their principals (United States Department of Education, 1996; Bookbinder, 1992; Sybouts & Wendel, 1994), it is necessary to identify and assess the degree to which various factors contribute to the success of secondary school principals.

Research Questions

The following four research questions were designed based on the four main parts of Chapter 2, Literature Review as cited in Lopez (1998). (1) Motivation, (2) Leadership, (3)

Successful Principals, and (4) Development of Successful Principals.

Research Question

What are the characteristics that contribute to the success of secondary school principals?

Subquestions

(1) What is the impact of motivation on the role relationship of principals?
(2) How do leadership styles contribute to the development of successful principals?
(3) What factors contribute to the development of principals' success?

Population and Sample

This research was conducted in Rhode Island and data were collected from a purposive sampling of 20 principals from the various school systems. The 20 principals were selected based on recommendation from their superintendents as having met the criteria established by the particular district. Some of these principals in the study are known as "distinguished principals" in Rhode Island and they are often selected to be mentors to aspiring principals. Each of these principals was invited to participate and they were provided with the purpose and further information regarding the study. The fact that this sample size was drawn from different school systems provided the researcher an opportunity to interview participants while they were involved in social practices at their schools.

Research Design

A qualitative method was used to investigate the problem of this study, which is to determine what factors contribute to the success of secondary school principals.

(1) A list of questions was developed based on Lopez (1998). The questions were asked based on the four parts of Chapter 2, Literature Review (Motivation, Leadership, Successful Principals, and Development of Successful Principals).
(2) Twenty successful principals were selected from the various school districts in Rhode Island as follows:

The researcher made phone calls to each of the superintendents of the various school districts in Rhode Island, and requested the names of their successful principals. These principals (N= 20) were selected on the basis of the standards and criteria set forth by the superintendent of the respective school districts. For example, some of these superintendents based the success of their principals on the extent to which they were able to fulfill the nine high performing standards set by the *Hope for Urban Education.* The school system that set standards based on *Hope for Urban Education,* also set standards based on a research study by the *Educational Trust.* Primary emphasis was placed on visionary leadership as the foundation pertaining to success for secondary school principals.

Another school district in Rhode Island selected their successful principals based on the *Ontario Institute Model.* This model allows the principals to use a rubric to conduct a self - assessment by presenting goal setting skills, action steps and indicators of accomplishment. Other school districts were influenced by the *Elementary and Middle*

Schools Proficiencies for Principals established by the *National Association of Elementary School Principals.* These school districts also incorporated the ISLLC standards.

(3) Based on the names provided to the researcher by the superintendents, phone calls were made to these principals, requesting permission to interview them on - site at their respective schools. All twenty principals agreed to be interviewed.

(4) The researcher met with these principals and reviewed the protocol for the interview and the purpose of the study (to determine the factors that led to their success). Participants voluntarily signed consent forms agreeing to be interviewed and to permit audio taping of the interview.

(5) Twenty similarly structured interviews were conducted at each individual principal's school, following a review of protocol and audio - taping procedures. The researcher asked a series of questions (See Appendix E) based on Lopez's (1998) study. Additional questions were developed during the interview in order for the researcher to have a deeper understanding of the discussion with the participants.

(6) Each of the twenty interviews was audio tape recorded (Creswell, 1994) and the researcher took field notes throughout each interview. Such information included notes on body language, so as to record observations about the congruence between what the participant discussed and the information his or her body language conveyed.

(7) Following each interview, audio - taped data were reviewed, (Creswell, 1994).

Anecdotal notes were collected, organized, analyzed and compared to establish a pattern.

(8) The data analysis process included the identification of themes that would contribute to clear understand of factors that contribute to success of principals.

This was accomplished by comparing each written transcript and the field notes, sorting data by interview question and by categories that developed in situ, and reporting and analyzing the data.

(9) The audio - tapes were placed in a secure file with printed copies of their transcripts.

Instrumentation

Prior to conducting the face - to - face interviews, protocols were written to ensure consistency and integrity of the information collected. All participants signed a letter of consent indicating that they understood the purpose of the study. The researcher assured anonymity and explained that participant data were to be presented by job classification.

A combination of in - depth and semi - structured interviews were used to collect data to answer the primary question. The interview process afforded the researcher an opportunity to guide the initial line of questioning and to probe for deeper meaning and clarity. The researcher developed interview questions based on the literature review (See Appendix E) In - depth interviewing also allowed the researcher "to ask participants to reconstruct their experience and to explore their meaning" (Seidman, 1998, p.76).

The researcher observed the participants during the interviewing, thus, the researcher was able to take anecdotal notes as an additional means of collecting data. The researcher used these anecdotal notes during the interviewing process to encourage participant reflection and exploration of those areas which participants found uncomfortable to discuss. In addition, the interviewer recorded notes on participant body language. Table 1 explains how interview questions were cross - referenced with research questions in order to observe the emerging patterns and themes from the responses.

Table 1

Interview Questions and Corresponding Research Questions	
Interview Question	**Corresponding Research Questions**
Describe the educational background that prepared you for the principalship.	What are the characteristics that contribute to the success of principals?
How many years have you been a principal?	*
What do you attribute to your effectiveness as a principal?	*
When do you feel satisfied at work?	*
What motivated you to become a principal?	What is the impact of motivation on the role of principals?

Table 1 Continued

Interview Questions and Corresponding Research Questions	
Interview Question	**Corresponding Research Questions**
When do you feel a sense of accomplishment?	*
What strategies do you have in place to motivate others within your learning community?	*
How would your school community characterize your assets as a leader?	How do leadership styles contribute to the to the success of secondary school principals?
Discuss your leadership styles and what you believe makes you successful as a leader.	*
How do others perceive you as a leader?	*
What new skills do you believe you will need to acquire for leadership in a 21st century school?	What are the factors that contribute to the development of successful principals?
How are you enhancing your knowledge and implementation of best practices?	*
As a principal, what role do you play in change and reform?	*
What would you distinguish as top priority in your role as principal?	What are the factors that contribute to the development of successful principals?
What role do critical friends play in your role as principal?	*
What systems do you have in place to acquire knowledge?	*

Table 1 Continued

Interview Questions and Corresponding Research Questions	
Interview Question	**Corresponding Research Questions**
What are the factors that have contributed to your growth and development?	*
How do you seek support for development as a principal?	*
What **are** your future plans for enhancing your leadership and role as a principal?	*

The Interviewing Process

The interview process consisted of three parts: Introduction, Questioning, and Wrap-Up.

Introduction

At the beginning of the session, the researcher introduced herself to the principals and briefly reviewed the purpose of the interview and the interview protocol. The researcher ensured that all the participants had read and signed the letter of consent The researcher reminded the participants that they could refrain from answering any question which made them feel uncomfortable. Each of the 20 interview sessions ran for 45 minutes.

Questioning

Questions were organized into four categories: Characteristics of Successful Principals, Motivation and the Role Relationship of Principals, Leadership Styles of Principals, and Factors that Contribute to the Development of Successful Principals (Lopez, 1998). At the beginning of each interview, the researcher reviewed the procedures for audio - taping before the taping session began. The investigator also reminded the participants that the session was to be semi - structured with prepared questions and questions that developed in situ, and they were at liberty to interrupt the taping session if they felt uncomfortable about a particular question.

The procedure for each session was as follows: The researcher read the question and then waited for a response from the participant. The researcher did not interpret any question but did probe for further information by asking participants to elaborate, complete or clarify their responses.

The presence of a tape recorder did not cause any obstruction and the participants reported that they felt completely comfortable as they responded to questions posed by the researcher.

Wrap-Up

Each interview was conducted within a 45 minute period. Toward the end of each session, the investigator announced the final question, allowing time to gather data. The investigator ended by thanking the participants.

Questions

The researcher asked twenty two prepared questions developed by Lopez (1998), (See Appendix E). These questions were based on the literature review for this study.

The questions focused on Motivation, Leadership, Successful Principals, and Development of Successful Principals. Probing questions developed in situ.

Data Collection Procedures

Although interviewing was the primary method for collecting data, in - depth information was also obtained through audio - taped interviews and through the additional notes the investigator took during the session. The emerging themes were then coded and categorized on response forms, according to the four parts of the literature review, which are (a) Characteristics of Successful Principals, (b) Motivation, (c) Leadership Styles, and (d) the Development of Successful Principals.

Data Analysis

Miles and Huberman (1994) recommend that data analysis occur concurrently with data collection. They further suggested that early data analysis allows the researcher to "cycle back and forth between thinking about the existing data and generating strategies for collecting new, often better, data" (p. 50). The taped interviews were transcribed and the notes were reviewed for the patterns of the four basic themes as based on the research questions and these are: (a) Characteristics That Contribute to the Success of Principals, (b) The Impact of Motivation on the Role Relationship of Principals, (c) Leadership Styles That Contribute to the

Success of Principals (d) Factors that Contribute to the Development of Successful Principals.

In order to facilitate the data analysis, the researcher developed a matrix (See Table 2). The matrix featured the four research questions as aligned with the themes of Motivation, Leadership, Successful Principals and the Development of Successful Principals.

Table 2

	Data Analysis Matrix Question		Themes	Findings	Discussion
Motivation	What impact does motivation play on the role relationship of principals?	Instructional Leader Manager Other			
Leadership	What impact does leadership have on the role relationship of principals?	Instructional Leader M nager Other			
Characteristics of Successful Principals	What are the characteristics that contribute to the success of principals and how do they develop those qualities and characteristics?	Instructional Leader Manager Other			
Development of Principals	What are the factors that contribute to the development of successful principals?	Instructional Leader Manager Other			

Twenty separate transcripts were created based on each participant's audio - taped responses. These transcripts were created to enable the researcher to examine the responses and the emerging themes from all four domains of the research questions. In the areas of Characteristics of Successful Principals, and Leadership the responses were aligned with qualities and characteristics of the contemporary leadership theories. These include Theory X, Theory Y, Transformational Leadership, Moral Leadership, and Empowered Leadership. All twenty two interview questions were converted into a matrix by aligning each research question with the responses given by the participants.

Through in - depth questioning, additional questions emerged in situ and corresponding data were merged as appropriate. Notes about the participants' body language were recorded in a notebook and it provided deeper meaning to the responses. The implications of the body language will be discussed in detail when the findings for this study are discussed.

The last interview question was in regard to the skills needed for secondary school principals in the 21st century. The researcher analyzed the skills needed, the kinds of resources principals will have to access, and the networking they will be involved in, if necessary.

Summary

Chapter 3, Methodology, began with an introduction and a restatement of the problem of this exploratory study, which investigated the factors that contributed to the success of secondary school principals. The research questions were presented. This Methodology section also described the qualitative procedures and the methods used in analyzing the data. Table 1 describes how the interview questions cross - referenced with the research questions. This table demonstrated that the questions asked during the interviews, were specific attempts to answer the research questions. Tables were used to explain how the emerging themes from the data analysis overlapped with the four areas of Motivation, Leadership, Successful Principals, and Development of Principals, which resulted in the findings that contributed to the success of secondary school principals.

CHAPTER FOUR

FINDINGS

Introduction

The purpose of this study was to examine the impact of factors that contribute to the success of secondary school principals in Rhode Island. Qualitative methodologies were explored to investigate the study's research question:

(1) What are the characteristics that contribute to the success of secondary school principals?
(2) What is the impact of motivation on the role relationship of principals?
(3) How do leadership styles contribute to the success of secondary school principals?
(4) What factors contribute to the development of principals' success?

This chapter will (a) Review the population and sample for the study, (b) Discuss the instrumentation used for the study, (c) Describe the data collection methodology, and (d) Present and discuss the findings.

Population and Sample

The research was conducted in Rhode Island public school system. Twenty secondary school principals were selected based on the recommendation made by the superintendents. The superintendents identified principals they considered to be successful, as determined by the evaluation system used at that particular school. While evaluative criteria for principals differ in each school system, all principals were required to work with interns and all were identified as " distinguished principals." Each principal recommended by a superintendent, was personally contacted by telephone and interview arrangements were made with them.

Instrumentation

Questions

The researcher asked the twenty-two interview question (Appendix E) developed by Lopez (1998). The interview questions investigated (a) Characteristics that Contribute to the Success of Secondary School Principals, (b) Motivation, (c) Leadership, and (d) Factors That Contribute to the Development of Principals. The interview questions were developed purposely in five categories Lopez (1998): (a) Experience and Behavior (b) Opinion and Value, (c) Feeling and Knowledge (d) Sensory Perceptions and (e) Background and Demographics (Patton, 1980).

Interview Process

Introduction

The researcher introduced herself to each principal and announced the purpose of her visit The researcher assured that the principals read and sign the consent forms. The researcher discussed the interviewing process protocol with each principal and explained that they could decline any questions with which they were uncomfortable, and reminded the participants that the session was to be audio - recorded. The researcher asked each of the twenty - two questions in Appendix E, allowing time for the principals to reflect on the question and to respond. The researcher probed for deeper meaning as necessary, based on the participant's response.

Questioning

The questions were organized into four categories to explore the characteristics of successful secondary school principals, and three motivation, leadership, and development of successful principals. The researcher read one question at a time and then waited for the participant's response. The researcher used a notebook to record data about the participant's body language and other comments of the participant for example, the researcher made notes of which questions participants felt animated and relaxed when they gave responses. The audio—taping also occurred simultaneously.

Wrap - Up

Each similarly structured interview took approximately, forty-five minutes. At the end of the questioning, the researcher asked the participant to offer any additional information they thought pertinent. The researcher ended the session by thanking the participants and later, a note of appreciation was sent to them.

Research Findings

Research uestion # 1

What are the characteristics that contribute to the success of secondary school principals?

A number of studies suggest that the principal' s most significant role is in the improvement of students' achievement. Other critical roles including serving as instructional leaders, managers of the building, and also as a liaison between the school and central administration, and between the school and the community. A review of the literature also revealed that successful principals must possess the following skills: (a) Good communication skills, (b) General intelligence, (c) High motivation, (d) Initiative, (e) Enthusiasm and self - confidence (f) Organization and follow through, and (g) Decision making and technical skills (law, budget, finance, and technology (Hart & Bredson, 1996; Richardson, et al., 1993; Depree, 1987; Sybouts & Wendel, 1994).

Research Question# 1 was designed to (a) Understand specific qualities and characteristics of successful principals and (b) Understand how they develop these qualities and characteristics (Lopez, 1998). Three specific questions in the area of characteristics that contribute to successful principals were asked. The three questions that corresponded with Research Question # 1 are the following:

(a) Describe the educational background that prepared you for the principalship?
(b) How many years have you been a principal? (c) What do you attribute to your effectiveness as a principal? and (d) When do you feel satisfied at work?

(See Table 3).

Table 3

Characteristics that Contribute to the Success of Secondary School Principals				
Interview Question# 1				
Describe the educational background that prepared you for the principalship.	10% of the participants (N= 2) principals reported that their educational experience provided them with solid foundation in school legal issues	100% of the participants (N = 20) principals reported that mentorship made it possible for them to form strong network of support	10% of the participants (N = 2) reported that internship gave them the opportunity to learn about the principalship	10% of the participants (N=2) reported that internship gave them the opportunity to learn about the principalship

Table 3 Continued				
Characteristics that Contribute to the Success of Secondary School Principals				
Interview Question #2 How many years have you been a principal?	Approximately 40% of the participants (N = 8) reported that they have been principals for at least 2 years	Approximately 40% of the participants (N = 8) reported they have been principals for at least 4 years	Approximately 10% of the participants (N = 2) have been in the position for at least 6 years	Approximately 10% of the participants (N = 2 have been principals for more than 9 years
Interview Question #6 When do you feel satisfied at work?	100% of the participants (N = 20) reported they felt satisfied when they observe that their students are happy and successful at what they do	100% of the participants (N = 20) reported they felt satisfied when students performed well on standardized tests	5% of the participants (N = 1) reported that he felt satisfied when students from this school are seen as products of a recognizable good school	5% of the participants (N = 1) reported that he felt satisfied when community members and stakeholders are delighted with what is going on in the school
Interview Question # 15 Asa principal, what role do you play in school change and reform?	JOO% of the participants (N = 20) reported that the principal played a major role in school by staying current with initiatives	100% of the participants (N = 20) reported they played a major role in the professional development for teachers	100% of the participants (N = 20) reported they were seen as instructional leaders by promoting students' learning	90% of the participants (N = 18) reported that they played a major role by staying connected with professional organizations

Table 3 Continued				
Characteristics that Contribute to the Success of Secondary School Principals				
Interview Question #16				
What would you distinguish as top priority in your role as principal?	100% of the participants (N = 20) reported that focusing on students' work was their top priority	85% of the participants (N = 17) reported forming strong relationships made them successful	100% of the participants (N = 20) reported that providing support for teachers was pivotal in their being successful as principals	100% of the participants (N = 20) reported that focusing on teaching and learning was their top priority

Findings

Emerging themes that resulted from questions relating to Research Question # 1 are as follows:

Instructional Leader

(1) Focus on the success of students
(2) Focus on Teaching and Learning
(3) Appropriate Professional Development **for** teachers
(4) Being a role model as a lead learner by attending workshops meant for the development of teachers

Organizational Leader

(1) Setting a vision for the school
(2) Empowering teachers so that they can be motivated to try new methods of teaching and learning
(3) Engaging parents in the spirit of the school by including them in activities

Table 4

Characteristics that Contribute to the Success of Secondary School Principals

Instructional Leadership

Principals reported that they made strong connections with students by the following:

Focusing on students' work

Getting involved in discipline

Learning the names of the students

Making a presence at **all** the lunches at the cafeteria

Working closely with parents

Recognizing students' achievement

Focusing on Teaching and Learning

Helping to provide a safe and orderly environment

Helping teachers to improve their teaching strategies

Increasing the knowledge and learning of teachers

Securing Resources

Making funds available to teachers

Securing resources from various sources

Support for Teachers

Maintaining an open - door policy with teachers

Being accessible to teachers

Forming strong relationships with teachers

Providing emotional support for teachers

Discussion

All twenty principals accepted and modeled the premise that the principal must serve as instructional leader. All participants agreed that successful principals help teachers and focus on students. In addition, all twenty principals indicated that their top priority in their role as principal was geared toward students' achievement.

In answering the question " What are the characteristics that contribute to the success of secondary school principals?" 90% of the participants reported that the major characteristics of successful principals were promoting students' learning, and supporting teachers in their teaching by providing them with the necessary resources. A review of the literature for this study also revealed that principals must possess the following skills: General intelligence, good communication skills, motivation, enthusiasm and self - confidence. Although 100% of the participants mentioned the fact that good communication skills are a necessary asset, none of them mentioned that the successful principal has to be intelligent.

Research Subquestion # 1
What is the impact of motivation on the role relationship of principals?

Three interview questions were asked in connection with this research questions and they were: (a) What motivated you to become a principal? (b) When do you feel a sense of accomplishment? (c) What strategies do you have in place to motivate others within your learning community? The data from the twenty principals interviewed was gathered, organized, and analyzed. Specific themes emerged: (a) Instructional Leadership, (b) Principals as Change Agents for Reform Agendas by Providing Strong, Leadership, and (c)

Support for Teachers and Other Staff Members. Ninety percent of the principals were motivated by the fact that they believed that they had a major contribution to make to education, and to the lives of children. They agreed that motivation played a major role in encouraging teachers to continue to work hard.

Findings

The themes that emerged from this data are the following:

Instructional Leadership

The participants reported that they were motivated to be involved in the principalship because it gave them the opportunity to be directly involved in education, thereby, impacting the lives of students. The principalship also gave school leaders the power to secure the necessary resources for the school. It also gave them the opportunity to form strong relationships within the school system.

Some of the responses fell under Organizational Behavior which led to: Building School Culture, and included the following:

- Vision and goal setting
- Empowerment
- General Leadership
- Focusing on parent and community partnerships
- Developing a community of leaders
- Implementing change and reform in instruction
- The above information is presented in Table 5

Table 5

Motivation: Emerging Themes
Forming strong connections with students by visiting classrooms and also being in the lunchrooms
Providing the necessary after school programs for students to enhance their learning
Providing teachers with the right resources so the teaching and learning can be an engaging activity.
Showing great interest in students' activities
Support for Teachers
Acknowledging teachers for good performance on the job
Showing great interest in teachers' welfare and emotional problems
Relationships
Maintaining very good interpersonal relationships with staff throughout the building.
Making a point to let teachers know you truly care about them
Organizational Leader
Building a school culture
Building school pride
Vision and Goal Setting
Keeping the vision in focus all the time
Vision and Goal Setting
Setting achievable goals
Setting clear expectations
Knowing the climate of the school
Sense of Accomplishment
Receiving compliments from colleagues
Receiving compliments from parents
Receiving note of thanks form parents

Discussion

Approximately N = 14 of the principals felt they had a very strong role to play in instructional leadership. They were motivated to become principals because they felt that the role of a principal would give them the power to influence how children learn and the extent to which they learn, thus, making a difference in education. N = 13 of the participants, echoed their deep interest in children and the desire to see them succeed in life.

The next theme that emerged is under organizational leadership. This accounts for personal background, prior experiences, diverse abilities, and teaching experience that motivated them to become principals. In the same way, principals used these factors to motivate teachers an other school personal at their schools. N = 5 of the participants indicated the factors listed above were some of the issues that motivate them to become principals.

N = 5 of the participants mentioned management as a motivating factor for them to be in the principalship. Management included schedules, finance, budgets and politics.

Research Subquestion # 2

How do leadership styles contribute to the success of secondary school principals? The interview questions asked in relation to this research questions were as follows: (a) Discuss your leadership style and what you believe makes you a successful as a leader. (b) How would your school community characterize your assets as a leader? (c) What new skills do you believe you will need to acquire for leadership in a 21st century school? Data gathered from the interview sessions were analyzed and categorized in Table 6. The themes that emerged were as follows: (a) Principal as collaborator (b)

Principal as capacity builder (c) Principal as instructional leader and (d) Principal as organizational leader.

Table 6

	How do Leadership Styles Contribute to the Development of Successful School Principals			
Interview Question # 10	Principal as Collaborator	Principal as Capacity Builder	Principal as Instructional Leader	Principal as Organizational Leader
Discuss your leadership style and what makes you successful as a leader	100% (N =20) of the participants reported this to be a trait of the successful principal	100% (N=20) of the participants reported they believed in empowering teachers to be leaders	90% (N =19) of the participants reported they believed this to be one of the traits of a successful principal	100% (N =20) of the respondents reported that the principal has to be accessible and knowledgeable about what goes on in the school
Interview Question #11	Principal as Collaborator	Principal as Capacity Builder	Principal as Instructional Leader	Principal as Organizational Leader
How do others in your school perceive you as a leader?	95% (N = 19) of the principals believed they are perceived as fair, honest, dependable and people - oriented	90% (N = 18) of the participants reported they try to encourage teachers to assume different roles at school	90% (N = 18) reported they are perceived as promoters of good instruction	100% (N = 20) reported that perceived as cheer leaders for their schools by promoting the positive aspects of the school

Table 6 Continued

How do Leadership Styles Contribute to the Development of Successful School Principals?

Interview Question # 12				
How do others in your school community characterize your assets?	50% (N = 10) reported that the principal is viewed as a leader who is constantly involving the larger community in school affairs	50% (N = 10) reported that they are perceived as encouraging teachers to take on leadership roles	90% (N = 18) reported they are perceived as involved in education and being the leaders of instruction	75% (N = 15) of the participants reported they are perceived as bridge builders between the school and the community
Interview Question # 13	**Principal as Collaborator**	**Principal as Capacity Builder**	**Principal as instructional Leader**	**Principal as Organizational Leader**
What new skills do you need to acquire for leadership in a 21st century school?	100% of the participants (N = 2) reported they needed more knowledge in technology so that they can communicate faster with teachers	75% of the participants (N = 15) reported they believed they would be modeling good behavior to teachers if they use technology effectively	50% of the participants (N = 10) reported that they believed they can generate and interpret data effectively with very good use of technology	5% of the participants (N = 1) reported that personal mastery of technology use will encourage other staff members to do the same

Findings

Emerging themes impacting the role relationship of principals as presented in Table 6, are explained as follows:

Principal as Collaborator

(1) Principal uses transformational style of leadership to include teachers, students, parents and other school personnel in what goes on at the school.
(2) Principal collaborates so that teachers, parents and students can have ownership in reform agendas at the school.
(3) Principal listens to ideas from teachers and other stakeholders in order to make reasonable changes where necessary.

Principal as Capacity Builder

One of the dominant themes is the fact that the principal who engages in collaboration build capacity. As one principal succinctly stated " I should feel comfortable that the work I have started will go on, if I should walk away from it tomorrow."

Instructional Leadership

(1) Presenting oneself as very knowledgeable in all areas of learning
(2) Collaborating with teachers to bring out the best in their teaching
(3) Focus on students' work

(4) Focusing on students' during standardized testing period and providing them support
(5) Focusing on securing resources for teachers
(6) Providing support for teachers
(7) Forming strong relationships with teachers

Principal as Organizational Leader

(1) Building school pride
(2) Keeping school vision in focus
(3) Empowering teachers to become leaders
(4) Providing general leadership in all areas of the learning community
(5) Forming strong parent and community partnerships
(6) Implementing change
(7) Networking with other principals
(8) Serving as lead learner
(9) Setting the example as a leader by modeling appropriate behavior
(10) Attending workshops presented to teachers

Discussion

In response to the question "How do leadership styles contribute to the success of secondary school principals?" Approximately 75% of the participants said they believed that a successful leader must be seen as an excellent collaborator. In achieving that goal, the leader must be a very good communicator in order to be able to relay new instructional practices effectively to other staff members. 50% (N =10) of the participants also believed that the success of leadership depends on modeling exemplary behavior and this is achieved by being accessible, visible, fair, strong, honest and he or she should have the ability to adapt to changing situations.

Approximately 5% (N =l) of the participants echoed the phrase "Don't ask teachers to do something you are not willing to do."

All twenty respondents agreed that the successful principal has to be motivated enough to provide general leadership in the school. They should be able to provide this type of strong leadership because of their background experiences, diverse abilities, teaching experiences, and relationships with other people. They concluded that any principal who promotes their type of leadership should be able to move the school toward a positive direction.

In analyzing the answers to the questions that related to the research question, "What is the impact of motivation on the role relationship of principals?" none of the respondents asserted that they were motivated to become a principal because they wanted to perform managerial duties. The participants agreed that they had to finalize budgets, schedules, finances, and deal with politics of the school as well as mandates from the State Department of Education, but their primary goal was to make an impact on teaching and learning. The fact that the participants had to perform all these functions, in addition to being instructional leaders, leaves researchers wondering about the type of impact such a load will have upon the principals.

It is quite obvious that the principals in this study have students' achievement as their central focus. They were motivated by external values like rewards from the community and acknowledgment from parents and stakeholders.

Forming Strong Connections with Parents and the Community

Many of the responses about how Leadership Styles Contribute to the Success of Principals included details about parent and community relations in addition to leadership provided within the school. Approximately, 95% (N =19) of the participants believed that the school leader must be seen as a liaison between the larger community and the school. For example, they must have the ability to make parents feel very welcome and comfortable at their schools.

In analyzing the responses in regard to leadership, none of the participant mentioned management as a contributing factor to the success of a secondary school principal. However, in describing their leadership styles, 100% (N = 20) did mentioned but did not emphasize management functions. Most of them described roles in relation to the school leader being an instructional leader and being a facilitator for learning. The principals also viewed themselves as the cheerleaders for their schools and they presented a very positive image of their schools. 100% reported they portrayed this image by forming very strong alliances within the school community and being visible within the school and the community.

Research Subquestion # 3

What are the factors that contribute to the development of successful principals? This question was designed to (a) Understand specific qualities and characteristics of successful principals, and (b) Understand how the principal develop these qualities and characteristics. Seven specific questions were asked during the interviews in relation to this research question and they are the following: (a) How are you enhancing your knowledge and implementation of best practices? (b) What would you distinguish as top priority in your role as principal? (c) What role do critical friends play in your role as principal, **(d)** What systems do you have in place to acquire knowledge? (e) What are the factors that have contributed to your growth and development? (f) How and where do you seek support for your development as a principal? and (g) What are your future plans for enhancing your leadership and your role as a principal?

Table 7

What are the Factors that Contribute to the Development of Successful Principals?				
Interview Question# 14				
How are you enhancing your knowledge and implementation of best practices?	75% of the participants (N = 15) reported that they network with various professional organization	80% of the participants (N = 16) reported they kept reading professional journals	80% of the participants (N = 16) reported they attended conferences and meetings within their districts	80% of the participants (N = 16) attended workshops designed for teachers 8

Table 7 Continued

What are the Factors that have Contribute to the Development of Successful Principals?				
Interview Question #17 What role do critical friends play in your role as principal	100% of the participants (N =20) reported that critical friends provided a knowledge base for them	Approximately 60% of the participants (N = 12) reported that friends served in a supportive and emotional role	Approximately 5% of the participants (N = 1) reported that they have a cohort of friends they approach for support	Approximately 50% of the participants (N = 10) reported that critical friends help them to sort out perplexing issues
Interview Question # 21 How and when do you seek development as a principal?	Approximately 75% of the participants (N = 15) reported they sought help from their colleagues	Approximately 15% of the participants (N = 3) reported that they received support from their spouses	50% of the participants (N = 10) reported they sought help from teachers	5% of the participants (N = 1) reported they received help from outside
Interview Question # 22 What are your plans for enhancing your leadership and your role as principal?	Approximately 90% of reported they planned on leaving the position because they are almost at the end of their career	5% (N= 1) reported they planned on becoming a superintendent	5% of the participants (N = 1) reported they would like to be in a position to help principals with professional development	5% of the participants (N = 1) reported they will like to go back to school for advanced degrees

Findings

The data provides evidence that both informal and formal opportunities contribute to the development of principals. Such opportunities include teacher evaluations which help inform professional and relationships with family, spouses, peers and personal support systems.

Approximately 80% (N = 16) of the principals contended that the success of secondary school principals is also attributed to their own personality and character, listening to ideas from other people, networking with peers, working long hours, and having endless energy and perseverance.

Additional contributing factors include partnerships with universities, connecting with university professors and other professional groups like the *National Association of Secondary School Principals, the Rhode Island Association of Administrators,* and attending conferences and area meetings with other principals.

Of principals interviewed, 75% (N = 15) reported they gained development opportunities through informal association within and outside schools. With reference to professional development, 25% (N = 5) of the respondents reported that they benefited from professional association, attending conferences, maintaining very good relationships with the superintendent of schools, engaging in professional development for administrators, and serving as mentors for aspiring principals. 75% (N =15) of the respondents admitted that they found it very enlightening to be connected with aspiring principals because it gave them the opportunity to be reflective in their practice. This information is reflected in Table 8.

Table 8

Development of Secondary School Principals		
Development Activities	Formal development opportunities	Informal development opportunities
Within School	Evaluating teachers Providing professional development for teachers	Supportive staff Maintain very good relations with the teachers' union representative
Within School	Assisting teachers to follow reform agendas of the school district	
Outside School Independent	Professional conferences Professional Organization Professional development Discussion groups Area meetings Have a good Assistant Superintendent	Serve community as a leader Network with other administrators Relationship with spouse Supportive family Meeting with experts in the field Personal support systems Listening to ideas Perseverance Endless energy Books Internet Traveling Extra curricula activities Background experiences Intuition Self - confidence

Discussion

The following theme emerged from the data from the interview question which asked "What new skills do you believe you will need to acquire for the leadership in a 21st century school?" Approximately, 95% (N = 19) of the participants reported that they needed more knowledge in the area of technology. 75% (N = 15) reported they needed to find a more effective way of using technology. 95% (N = 19) felt that the skills they had described in the other three research questions most of the skills needed for the 21st century secondary school principal.

Summary

Research question relating to the factors that contribute to the development of secondary school principals revealed the following major theme.

(1) Principals' professional development tends to occur largely through informal means and informal associations.
(2) Principals' professional development occurs mostly outside of school activities
(3) Principals' professional development of principals is usually occurs independently.

Chapter 4 presented the research findings as a result of the data gathered, analyzed, and organized for this study. The data were collected through the interviews with twenty secondary school principal. These participants were selected based on recommendations from superintendents who identified the participants as "distinguished principal." Following collection, the data were analyzed to determine emerging themes and frequency counts. The data were described both in narrative form, and through tables.

CHAPTER FIVE

SUMMARY, CONCLUSIONS, RECOMMENDATIONS, AND IMPLICATIONS FOR FUTURE RESEARCH

Introduction

Chapter Five consists of a statement of the purpose of the study, a summary of the research design, conclusions, recommendations, and implications for further research.

Purpose of the Study

There has been a renewed interest in the performance of schools since the publication of the *A Nation at Risk* (1983). This renewed interest in education has led to an abundance of research focused on effective schools, characteristics and skills of effective principals, and leadership. In fact, a number of studies identify the principal as the critical element in successful schools (Bookbinder, 1992; Levin, 1997; Lipham, 1981; Sybouts & Wendel, 1994).

Therefore, this study investigated the factors that contribute to the success of secondary school principals. Specifically, the study reviewed the impact of various factors in terms of their contribution to the success of principals. These factors include mentoring, training and development programs, alternate routes to certification, and personal reflection through the use of the *Interstate School Leaders Licensure Consortium* (ISLLC Standards).

As previously stated, the role of the secondary school principal has become precarious as indicated by the high attrition rate among secondary school principals. In fact Fullan (1997) states that "Despite all the attention on the principal's leadership role we appear to be losing ground, if we take as our measure of progress the declining presence of increasingly large numbers of highly effective, satisfied principals" (p. 1).

The present condition of the principalship is a result of the ever - increasing expectations being placed on principals (Fullan, 1997). There is no doubt that principals must assume a multifaceted role in schools. On one side, they are expected to lead an intricate organization dealing with budget, supervision, curriculum and instruction, parent and community development, and staff development. At the same time, they have to deal with major reforms required by central office administration, the governing board, and state and federal legislation. Principals are also expected to be instructional leaders, and to transform the world of teachers, parents and students through collaboration. "It takes both technical competence and symbolic sensitivity to get the job done with dignity and grace" (Deal & Peterson, 1994, p. 10).

A number of studies have been conducted concerning different aspects of the principalship. Educational Research has focused on principals as leaders; transformational leaders; principals as dynamic leaders; principals fostering empowerment; the principal and school effectiveness; leadership characteristics and school improvement, and many other related aspects of the principalship. "Unfortunately, the results of research on the principalship offer limited guidelines for those interested in improving the effectiveness of school site administrators" Bookbinder, 1992, p. 20). Thus, considering the current status of the principalship and the fact that there is limited research on improving the effectiveness of the principal, this study examined the factors that have contributed to the success of secondary school principals in Rhode Island.

Research Design

Research Questions

The primary research question of this study was designed by incorporating major findings from the literature review: (a) Characteristics of Successful principals, (b) The Impact of Motivation on the Role Relationship of principals, (c) Leadership Styles, and (d) the Development of Successful Principals. In order to come to an understanding as to why some principals are successful, the following questions were addressed in the study and through a review of the literature.

Research Question # 1

What are the characteristics that contribute to the success of secondary school principals?

Subquestions

- What is the impact of motivation on the role relationship of principals?

- How do leadership styles contribute to the development of successful principals?
- What factors contribute to the development of principals' success?

This exploratory study followed a qualitative research design, whereby the researcher conducted interviews with twenty principals in order to identify factors that contribute to the success of secondary school principals in Rhode Island. The data from the audio - taped interviews were supplemented with additional notes recorded by the researcher during the sessions. The data were analyzed, grouped and categorized. The emerging themes were then coded and categorized, and were reported in narrative form with supporting tables.

Corroborating Literature

The literature review offered a number of theories of motivation, and provided a rational of why individuals strive to achieve certain goals. The premise for this argument is the fact it takes real leadership to motivate people to excel. In that sense, leadership and motivation are intricately woven together. Findings from a number of studies of conducted during the mid part of the 20th century revealed that individuals in the work place settings are motivated by being part of the decision - making process and having a sense of ownership over their work (Lopez, 1998). The principals interviewed in this study indicated that they collaborate with their staff for this reason.

A review of the literature regarding leadership revealed a historical perspective of leadership and several theories of leadership. Of significance, is the fact that many of the theories, such as transformational leadership, and empowerment suggests that the leader and the follower form a relationship to develop and self - actualize. These ideas align closely with Maslow's Hierarchy of Needs, and Herzberg's Two Factor Model which focuses on higher levels of self - esteem, self - actualization, and content satisfiers (achievement, recognition, responsibility, work itself, and advancement). The participants in this study reported that they support and empower their staff.

As the various leadership theories were explored, a link was established between leadership and motivation. One emerging theme in the literature is the importance of interaction with others, as leaders impact and influence the behavior of other people.

Sergiovanni (1996) argued that all theories of leadership aim at connecting people to each other, and all theories of leadership invariably lead to connecting people to their work.

The findings of this study suggest that successful principals can use such information to motivate staff members and hence lead to their own success.

This study's findings are also corroborated by literature concerning new roles for principals, suggesting that (a) The current crisis in the principalship is directly related to the new roles that have been thrust upon principals, (b) It will require a new and transformational view of leadership for any principal to be effective under the current paradigm, (c) An effective leader knows how to motivate other staff members, to and (d) A number of intricacies, roles, skills, behaviors and practices are required of successful principals.

The last section of Chapter Two investigated the development of principals, and it reviewed an area that had not been previously explored in school organizations; specifically investigating what factors contribute to the success of secondary school principals. This section undoubtedly dealt with the pivotal question, " what are the factors that contribute to the success of secondary school principals?

Conclusions

Summary of Findings

The following summary is presented per each research question.

Research Question # 1

What are the characteristics that contribute to the success of secondary school principals? Conclusions drawn from the findings demonstrate evidence of the following:

(1) Principals reported that the general leadership characteristics include being perceived as instructional leaders, that is, promoters of students' learning and supporting teachers in their teaching by providing them with the necessary resources.

(2) Principals also perceived themselves as organizational leaders, setting a vision for their schools.

(3) As part of their general leadership, principals perceived that they empower teachers through collaboration.

(4) They also viewed themselves as agents of change who promote reform agendas of the various districts.

(5) Personal qualities of possessing enthusiasm, motivation and self-confidence were all viewed as necessary character traits of a successful principal.

(6) Although general intelligence is clearly required of successful principals, none of the twenty principals who were interviewed identified it as one of their traits. The fact that it was not mentioned might be an indication that it is a trait all principals must have in order to take on such a monumental task.

Research Subquestion # 1

What is the impact of motivation on the role relationship of principals?

Themes regarding motivation and its impact on the role relationship of principals emerged from the data as follows:

(1) Principals reported they were perceived to present strong instructional leadership at their schools, thereby providing tremendous support for their students.
(2) Principals again reported being perceived as strong leaders by modeling good example to encourage teachers to work hard.
(3) The role for which principals seem to be least motivated was as a manager. None of the twenty participants mentioned the fact that they were motivated to become principals because they wanted to be managers of their schools

Research Subquestion # 2

How do leadership styles contribute to the success of secondary school principals?

The following theme were drawn from the findings for research subquestion number two.

(1) Principals were perceived to be collaborators, using this style to empower teachers.
(2) Principals reported they were viewed as capacity builders by sharing power with teachers.
(3) Principals were also viewed as instructional leaders by promoting good instruction through the efforts of teachers.

(4) Principals reported they were viewed as organizational leaders who were very knowledgeable about what goes on at the various schools.

Research Subquestion # 3

What are the factors that contribute to the development of successful Principals?

The emerging themes drawn from the findings of research subquestion # 3 is as follows:

(1) Principals are seen as capacity builders.
(2) Principals are also viewed as instructional leaders, presenting themselves as being very knowledgeable in all areas of learning, focusing on students' work, and securing the necessary resources for teachers.
(3) Principals reported that they are viewed as organizational leaders achieving this by building school pride, and keeping school vision in focus.
(4) Principals form strong parent and community partnerships, implementing change and networking with other principals
(5) Principals receive most of their development opportunities outside of their schools.
(6) Principals reported that some development opportunities were informal rather than formal. These informal opportunities came from colleagues, family members, spouses, and other individuals.

Principals reported that they needed most formal training in effective and efficient ways of using information and mandates from the federal and state levels.

Recommendations

This qualitative research study was conducted to investigate the factors that contribute to the success of secondary school principals in Rhode Island. Three research subquestions further directed the research:

(1) What is the impact of motivation on the role relationship of principals?
(2) How do leadership styles contribute to the success of secondary school principals?
(3) What are the factors that contribute to the development of successful principals?

Based on the findings and conclusions of this study, the following recommendations are offered to legislators, the Board of Education, superintendents, assistant superintendents principals, staff developers, educators, and other members of the learning community:

(1) Invest monetary and human resources in the professional development of principals, as this group of leaders is the pivotal factor in successful schools.
(2) Superintendents and assistant superintendents should offer continuous support in a non - threatening manner to both new and veteran principals. In other words, there should be a collegiality that transcends professionalism between the principal and the superintendent to help alleviate the pressure and the loneliness of the job.
(3) Principals should have time for informal development through networking with colleagues and building trusting relationships - that will help

minimize the unhealthy competition between secondary school principals.
(4) Principals should be given the opportunity to hand pick their administrative team so that they can work from the same philosophical base.
(5) Principals should be given additional support to work within the boundaries of mandates issued by both the federal government and the state for example, *(The No Child Left Behind Initiative)*, so as to mitigate additional pressure on principals.
(6) Principals should be given the support to build trusting relationships between the school and the communities, even if they do not live within the school district.
(7) Principals should be given release time to network and to bond with other principals.
(8) Principals should be given the necessary support in order to release them from operating both as managers and instructional leaders of their schools.

Implications for Future Research

As cited earlier, many studies have been conducted in the area of leadership, effective leadership and leadership styles but research is limited in terms of the professional development of successful principals. A number of studies focus on the shortage of principals, and the fact that schools are performing poorly because of ineffective principals. Thus, this research identified the factors that contribute to the success of principals in Rhode Island. Future research that will enhance the educational profession, leadership, and the development of principals include the following:

(1) Conduct a similar study with a different population.

(2) Conduct a similar study with a population of minority secondary school principals.
(3) Compare principals' personality profiles with their success as secondary school principals.
(4) Conduct a similar study with a comparison between principals who are trained by the traditional classroom methods and those who trained through the residency programs.

REFERENCES

Atkinson, J.W., & Birch, D. (1978). *Introduction to motivation.* New York: D. Van Nostrand Company.

Barth, R. (1991, March). A personal vision of a good school. *Phi Delta Kappan,* 71(7), 12 - 517.

Barth, R. (1990). *Improving schools from* within. San Francisco: Jossey- Bass, Inc. Barth, R. (2002, May). The culture builder. *Educational Leadership,* 59(8), 5 - 6.

Bennis, W., & Townsend, R. (1995). *Reinventing leadership.* New York: William Morrow & Company, Inc.

Bolman, L. G., & Deal. T. E. (1997). *Reframing organizations: Artistry, choice, & leadership.* (2nd ed.). San Francisco: Jossey - Bass Inc.

Bookbinder, R. (1992). *The principal.* Springfield, IL: Charles C. Thomas Publisher.

Bowen, D., Lewicki, R., Hall, D., & Hall, F., (1997). *Experiences in management and organizational behavior* (4th ed.). Canada: John Wiley & Sons, Inc.

Bums, J. (1978). *Leadership.* New York: Harper & Row.

Callahan, R. (1962). *Education and the cult of efficiency.* Chicago: The University of Chicago Press.

Checkley, K. (2000, May). The contemporary principal: New skills for a new age. *Educational Leadership, 42*(3), 1 - 8.

Covey, S. (1992). *Principal - Centered leadership.* New York: Simon & Schuster.

Crow, G. M., & Matthews, L. J. (1998). *Finding one's way: How mentoring can lead to a dynamic leader.* Thousand Oaks, CA: Sage.

Creswell, J. W. (1994). *Research design: Qualitative and quantitative approaches.* Thousand Oaks, CA: Sage.

Creswell, J. W. (2002). *Research Design: Qualitative, quantitative, and mixed methods approaches.* (2nd ed.). CA: Sage

Deal, T., & Peterson, K. (1994). *The Leadership paradox.* San Francisco: Jossey-Bass.

Daresh, J. (1990). Formation: The missing ingredient in administrator preparation. *National Association of Secondary School Principals Bulletin, 74*(526), 1 - 1.

Daresh, J., & Playko, M. (1992). Entry year programs for principals: Mentoring and other forms of professional development. *Catalyst, 21*(2), 24 - 29.

DePree, M. (1989). *Leadership is an art.* New York: Dell.

DuFour, R. (2002, May). The Learning - Centered principal. *Educational Leadership, 59*(8), 12 - 15.

Drucker, P. F., (1999). *Management challenges for the 2J8t century.* New York: Harper Collins Publishers, Inc.

Erickson, H. L., (1998) *Concept - Based curriculum and instruction: Teaching beyond the facts.* Thousand Oaks, CA: Sage Publications.

Evans, R. (1995, April 12). Getting real about leadership. *Education Week, 14*(29), p. 36

Ewing, T.M. (2001). Accountable leadership: The relationship of principal leadership style & student achievement in urban elementary schools. (Doctoral Dissertation, Northern Illinois University, 2001). *Dissertation Abstracts International,* 62, p. 4006.

Franklin, J (2000, December). Evaluating the school principal. Changing processes for changing roles. *Educational Leadership,* 42(8), 1 - 8.

Fullan, M. (1997). *What's worth fighting for in the principalship.* New York: Teachers College Press.

Fullan, M. (2002, May). The change leader. *Educational Leadership,* 59(8), 16 - 17.

Fullan, M. (1998, April). School leadership for the 21st century: Breaking the bonds of dependency. *Educational Leadership,* 55(7), 6 - 10.

Gardner, J. (1989, January). The moral aspects of leadership. *NASSP Bulletin.* 73(513), P. 43

Gall, M .D., Borg, W.R., & Gall, J.P. (1996). *Educational Research: An Introduction.* (6th ed). New York: Longman.

Gilman, D.A., & Givens, B. L. (2001, May). Where have all the principals gone? *Educational Leadership,* 58(8), 72-74.

Goertz, J. (2000). Creativity: An essential component for effective leadership in today's schools. *Roeper Review,* 23(3), 158-162.

Goldring, E. B. & Rallis, S. F. (1993). *Principals of dynamic schools: Taking Charge of change.* CA: Corwin Press.

Guzman, N. (1997) Leadership for successful inclusive schools: A study of principal behaviours. *Journal of*

Educational Administration. 35(5) 439 450. ERIC Document Reproduction Service no. EJ553868.

Hart, A, & Bredson, P. (1996). *The principalship -A theory of professional learning and Practice.* New York: McGraw-Hill, Inc.

Herzberg, F. (1959). *Motivation to* work. New York: John Wiley & Sons. Hershey, P., & Blanchard, K. (1993). *Management of organizational* behavior: Englewood Cliffs, NJ: Simon & Schuster.

Hershey, P., & Blanchard, K. (1982). *Management of organizational behavior: Utilizing human resources.* Englewood Cliffs, NJ: Prentice-Hall, Inc.

Hindrichs, J. (1974). *The motivation crisis.* New York: American Management Associations.

Johnson, N. A. (1993). The principal and school effectiveness: Principals' perspectives. *Journal of Personal Evaluation in Education,* 7(4), 339-354. ERIC Document Reproduction Service no. EJ478678.

Johnson, W. L. & Snyder, K. (1990, April). Instructional leadership training needs for educational administrators. *Presented at the Annual Meeting of the American Educational Association.* Boston, MA. ERIC Document Reproduction Service no. ED321378

Kazdin, A. E., (1994). *Behavior modification in applied setting.* Belmont, CA: Wadsworth, Inc.

Keller, B. (2000, May 3). Building on experience. *Education Week,* 19(34), p. 36 - 40. Kimbrough, R. B. & Burkett, C. W. (1990) *The Principalship: Concepts and practices.*

Needham Heights, MA: Allyn & Bacon.

Lashway, L. (1998, Winter). Measuring leadership. *Research Roundup National Association of Elementary School Principals,* 14(2), 1 - 5.

Levin, H. (1997, Fall/Winter). The Dilemma of principal succession. *Accelerated Schools.* (6)3, 1 - 2.

Licata, J.W. & Ellett, C.D. (1990). LEAD program provides support for the development of new principals. *NASSP bulletin,* 74(525), 5-10.

Lipman, J. (1981). *Effective principal, effective school.* Reston, VA: National Association of Secondary School Principals.

Loos, M. W. (2001). Improved Leadership through Myers-Briggs analysis: Personality styles of principals and teachers at secondary level. (Doctoral dissertation, University of San Francisco, 2001). *Dissertation Abstracts International,* 62, p. 3642

Lopez, P.E. (1998). Factors that Contribute to the Development of Effective Principals. (Doctoral dissertation, Northern Arizona University, 1998). *UMI:* 9918743

Love, D. W. (2000). The availability of qualified candidates for the secondary principalship in Arkansas. (Doctoral dissertation, University of Arkansas, 2000). *Dissertation Abstracts International,* 62, p. 1285.

Maslow, A. (1954). *Motivation and personality.* New York: Harper & Brothers. Mann, M. (1998). *Professional development for educational leaders.* Position Paper. ERIC Document Reproduction Service no. ED 415588.

McGregor, D. (1960). *The Human side of enterprise.* New York: McGraw-Hill. Merriam, S. B. (1998). *Qualitative research and case study applications in education.* San Francisco: Jossey-Bass publishers.

Miles, M. B., & Huberman. M.A. (1994) *Qualitative data analysis.* (2nded.). Thousand Oaks, CA: Sage.

Morise, D. (1990, May). An effective principal training and support system. *NASSP Bulletin.* 74(526).

National Association of Secondary school Principals (1978). *NASSP Assessor Handbook* Reston: VA: NASSP.

National Commission on Excellence in Education. (1983). *A nation at risk: The imperative for educational reform.* Washington, DC: No. 065-000-00177-2 Government Printing Office.

Owens, R. (1995). *Organizational behavior in education* Needham Heights. MA: Allyn & Bacon.

Owens, R. (1998). *Organizational behavior in education* (6th ed.). Needham Heights, MA: Allyn & Bacon.

Parks, D. (1991, December). Three Concepts Shape the New Roles of Principals in Administrator Preparation. *National Association of Secondary School Principals Bulletin.* 75(539), 8 - 12.

Porter, L. & Lawler, E. (1968). *Managerial attitudes and peiformance.* Homewood, IL: Richard D. Irwin, Inc.

Richardson, M., Short, P., & Prickett, R. (1993). *School principals and change.* New York: Garland Publishing, Inc.

Schmuck, RA (1993). *Beyond academic in the preparation of education leaders. Four years of action research.* 33(2). Oregon School Study Council. ERIC Document Reproduction Service no. ED 354610.

Schwahn, C., & Spady, W. (1998). *Total leaders: applying the best future jocused change strategies to education.* Arlington, VA: American Association of School Administrators.

Seidman, 1 (1998). *Interviewing as qualitative research. A guide for researchers in education and the social sciences.* New York: Teachers College Press.

Senge, P. (1990). *The fifth discipline: The art and practice of the learning organization.* New York: Doubleday/Currency.

Sergiovanni, T. J., (1996). *Leadership for the schoolhouse: How is it different? Why is it important?* San Francisco: Jossey - Bass Inc.

Short, P. M. (1998). Empowering leadership. *Contemporary Education,* 69(2), 70 - 72. ERIC Reproduction Service no. EJ564685.

Silins, H. C. (1994, November). Leadership characteristics and school improvement. *Australian Journal of Education,* 38(3), 266-281. ERIC Document Reproduction Service no.EJ496492.

Smith, W., & Andrews, R. (1989). *Instructional leadership: How principals make a difference.* Alexandria, VA: Association for Supervision and Curriculum Development.

Strodl, P. (1993). *Constituency Leadership: A model for school leaders.* Paper presented at the Annual Meeting of the Eastern Research Association (Clearwater Beach, FL), p. 1 - 8 ERIC Document Reproduction Service no. ED355615.

Stover, D. (1990, April). Education is getting serious about administrator preparation. *The Executive Educator.* 12(4), 18 - 20.

Sybouts, W., & Wendel, F. (1994). *The training and development of school principals.* Westport, CT: Greenwood Press.

Thody, A. (1997). *Leadership of Schools: Chief Executives in Education.* London: Redwood Books.

Tirozzi, G.N. (2001, February). The Artistry of leadership: The evolving role of the secondary school principal. *Phi Delta Kappan,* 82(6), 434 - 439.

Verona, G.S. (2001). The influence of principal transformational leadership style on high school proficiency test results in New Jersey comprehensive and vocational-technical high school. *Dissertation Abstracts International* 62(03A) p. 874.

Webb, L.D., & Norton, M.S. (1999). *Human resources administration: Personnel issues and needs in education.* Upper Saddle River, NJ: Prentice-Hall, Inc.

Whaley, M. (2002, January 24th). *Denver Post Education Writer.* Section: DTW, Article ID 108992, p. B - 02.

Yerkes, D. M. & Guaglianone, C. L. (1998). Recruiting and retaining effective high school administrators. National telephone interviews with practicing high school administrators. Unpublished raw data. *Presented at the Annual Conference of the Association of California School Administrators.* San Diego, CA

APPENDIX A

Johnson & Wales University
Feinstein Graduate School
Doctoral Program in Educational Leadership

Use of Human Subjects in Field Projects
and/or Dissertation Research

All students are required to submit this form as soon as their committee and the University Dissertation Review Committee have formally approved their dissertation proposal. This approval must be obtained before any substantive work is initiated on the dissertation. The signatures on this fonn signify sud approval. This form must be submitted to the Director of Research.

Student	Dinah A. Larbi
Home Address	139 Home Ave. Providence, R.I. 02908

Proposed Dissertation Topic	Factors that contribute to the success of Secondary School Principals

Projected Data Collection Period	From	January 2003	To	March 2003

The following questions must be addressed completely. Copies of the instrument(s) that will be used to gather data must accompany this form. Research application must include a consent statement or form appropriate to the research questions. (Use the sample form as a guide in preparing fonns, letters, and oral statements.) Research involving the use of existing data without identifiers does not require consent from subjects.

Abstract/Lay Summary

Describe the research, including research questions, the purpose of the research, and ihe methods to be used (hypothesis and methodology). Describe the task(s) subjects will be compleie. Use lay language (language understood by a person unfamiliar with the area of research). If using existing data or records, explain sources of data and the means of accessing the data. (Provide attachments as necessary.)

Subject Population

Subjects. Describe the subjects to be studied: number, gender, age range, location (e.g. elementary/secondary school, university, public institution, hospitals and clinics, private institutio;1, other). Describe any special characteristics of the subjects: (e.g., mentally/physically challenged, gifted and talented at risk, other).

The signatures below certify that:

- The information provided in the attached application form is correct.
- The principal investigator will seek and obtain prior written approval from the Program Director in the event of any substantive modification in the proposal, including, but not limited to changes in cooperating investigators and agencies, as well as changes in procedures.
- Unexpected or otherwise significant adverse events in the course of this study will be promptly reported.
- Any significant new findings that develop during the course of this'study which may affect the risks and benefits of participation will be reported in writing to the Program Director and to the subjects.
- The research may not and will not be initiated until final written approval is granted.

This research, once approved, is subject to continuing review and approval by the major advisor and the Director of the Doctoral Program. The principal investigator will maintain complete and accurate records of this research. If these conditions are not met, approval of this research could be suspended.

Student (Principal Investigator)		
Dinah A. LarbI	*[signature]*	3-7-03
Name	Signature	Date

As major advisor, I assume responsibility for ensuring that the principal investigator complies with University and federal regulations regarding the use of human subjects in research. I acknowledge that this research is in keeping with the standards set by the University and assure that the principal investigator has met all the requirements for approval of this research.

Major Advisor Dr. Lou D'Abrosca		
	[signature]	3/10/03
Name	Signature	Date

As Director of the Doctoral Program, I acknowledge that this research is in keeping with the standards set by the University and assure that the student has met all requirements for approval of this research.

Director		
	[signature]	3/19/03
Name	Signature	Date

Attached: Human Subjects Application

APPENDIX B

VINCENT A. CIANCI, JR.
Mayor

DIANA LAM
Superintendent

OUR SCHOOLS. OUR FUTURE.

SAMUEL W. BRIDGHAM
MIDDLE SCHOOL

Richard Cochran
Principal

Dinah Larbi
Assistant Principal

Robert Perkins
Assistant Principal

Ruth Berard
Director of Guidance

January, 8th 2003

Dear Dr. Nasif,

Thank you very much for taking the time to talk to me on January 6th 2003 - this is a follow up to the conversation. My name is Dinah Larbi and I am a former student of yours at Providence College, currently an Assistant Principal at Bridgham middle school in Providence.

Sir, I am in a doctoral program at Johnson & Wales in University and I am conducting a study on *Factors that contribute to successful secondary school principals in Rhode Island*, toward the writing of my dissertation. As part of my study, I would like to interview some of your *successful principals* about their practice, if it is alright with you. If you will do this, I will greatly appreciate it and thank you very much for your help and time.

Sincerely,

Dinah A. Larbi

Dinah A. Larbi

APPENDIX C

CONSENT FORM

Department of Educational Leadership
Program, Graduate School, Johnson & Wales University
Consent Form For *Factors that Contribute
to the Success of Secondary School
Principals: The Rhode Island Experience,*

I have been asked to take part in a research project which is going to determine the factors that contribute to successful principals in Rhode Island. The purposese of this study is to determine if there.are some unique factors that make these principals successful so the information can be used later. The researcher will explain the project to me in detail. I should feel free to ask questions. Ifl have further questions later, Dinah A. Larbi, the person mainly responsible for this study, will discuss them with me. Her telephone number is (401) 456-9360.

Description of the Project:
I have been asked to take part in a research study which is going to determine the factors that contribute to successful principals in Rhode Island. The purpose of this study is to use qualitative method to collect data from successful principals in Rhode Island.

What Will, Be Done:
This is an exploratory study and data will be collected through qualitative means and *interviewing* will be the primary tool for collecting data from participants. The study will take approximately three months. Data will be collected and analyzed from January until March 2003. The participants will be required to answer questions regarding their practice. Risks or Discomforts: There will not be any risks or discomforts associated with this study.

Benefits of This study:
Although there may be no direct benefits to ,me as a result of taking part in this study, I will get the opportunity to reflect on my study and the researcher will also have the opportunity to learn about what factors determines successful principals in Rhode Island.

Confidentiality:
My part in this research is confidential. None of the information will identify me by name. AU information will be given a code number. I know that the project director will have the code that links my name with the code number and access to the data will be limited to the research team. The data will be stored in a locked mJ and destroyed after the research has been concluded.

No information about you or your family will be given to anyone outside of the project team. The one exception to this confidentiality is that federal and state law mandates that we report to the authorities information that a child is being abused or is in imminent danger. Otherwise all information will be available only to research staff at Johnson & Wales University.

Voluntary Participation:

The decision whether or to take part in this research study is voluntary on my part. I do not have to participate. IfI do decide to take part in this study, I may terminate my participation at any given time. IfI wish to terminate my participation in the research study, I simply inform Dinah Larbi at (401) 456-9360 of my decision. What ever I decide will in no way affect my career.

Rights and Complaints:
IfI am not satisfied with-the way this study is performed or if I believe I have been injured in any way by participating in this study, I may conv y my concerns to Dinah A. Larbi at (401) 456-9360, anonymously ifI choose.

I may also write or call a representative of the Graduate School Institutional Review Board (IRB), AT Johnson & Wales University which oversees research involving human subjects. The Institutional Review Board may be reached at the following address: Johnson & Wales University Graduate School, IRB, 8 Abbott Park Place, Providence, RI 02903. You may contact the Board by telephone at (401) 598-1803.

I HAVE READ THE CONSENT FORM. MY QUESTIONS HAVE BEEN ANSWERED. MY SIGNATURE ON THIS FORM MEANS THAT I UNDERSTAND THE INFORMATION AND I CONSENT TO PARTICIPATE IN THIS STUDY.

Signature of Participant	Signature of Researcher
Typed/Printed Name of Participant	Typed/Printed Name of Researcher

CONSENT TO AUDIO-TAPING & TRANSCRIPTION

Factors that Contribute to the Success of Secondary School principals: The Rhode Island Experience

Dinah A. Larbi, Johnson & Wales University

I understand that this study involves audio taping of my interview with the researcher. Neither my name or any other identifying information will be associated with the audio tape or the transcript. Only the researcher will be able to listen to the tapes.

I understand that-the tapes will be transcribed by the researcher and erased once the transcriptions are checked for accuracy. Transcripts of my interview may be reproduced in whole or in part for the use of presentations or written products that result from this study. Neither my name nor any other identifying information (such as my voice or picture) will be used in presentations or in written prpducts resulting from this study.

Please check one of each pair of options.

- A. I consent to have my interview taped.-I do <u>not consent to have my interview taped.</u>
- B. I consent to have my taped interview transcribed into written form- I do <u>not consent to have my taped interview transcribed.</u>
- C. I consent to the use·of the written transcription in presentations and written products resulting from this study, provided that neither my name nor other identifying information will be associated with the transcript-or I do not consent to the use of my written transcription in presentations or written products resulting from this study.

The above permissions are in effect until May, 2003. On or before May 2003, the tapes will be destroyed.

Participants signature _____

I hereby agree to abide by the particippnts above instructions.

Researcher's signature _____

Date

APPENDIX D

THE EVALUATION PROCESS

Pre-Planning: Using the new Administrator Evaluation Form based on the Interstate School Leaders Licensure Consortium Standards for School Leaders and the accompanying rubric, the administrator and the evaluator will formally confer to review. clarify, and mutually agree to at least three performance goals. During this conference, clear expectations will be set regarding the objectives and action steps associated with the selected goals.

(Completed by November 15)

Action Phase: It is the responsibiiity of the administrator to collect evidence of work toward the established goals. The administrator and the evaluator will set up at least three visitation dates at the school during the academic year to discuss and review evidence of progress and accomplishments. At this time it would be appropriate to document any

necessary revisions to the goals based on changed or changing circumstances.
(Must occur between November 17 and May 15)

Evaluation Phase: The evaluator will make an appointment with the administrator to hold a comprehensive review of performance using the completed evaluation form and written summary. It is expected that each administrator will achieve a proficient rating or an average minimum of 3.0. A rating of less than proficient (3.0) in any one category may result a growth plan for the individual administrator as mutually agreed upon by the School Department and APPSSA.

(The final meeting must occur between May 16 and the last day of the academic school year)

APPENDIX E

THE INTERVIEW QUESTIONS

Interviewing will include the following questions, which will be based on the research questions and the literature review.

(1) Please describe the educational background that prepared you for the principalship.
(2) How many years have you been a principal?
(3) What motivated you to become a principal?
(4) To what do you attribute to your success as a principal?
(5) What drives you in perfonning your job as a principal?
(6) When do you feel satisfied at work?
(7) Who are you most satisfied working with?
(8) When do feel a sense of accomplishment?
(9) What strategies do you use to motivate others within your learning community?
(10) Discuss your leadership style and what you believe makes you successful as a leader.
(11) How do others in your school perceive you as a leader?
(12) How would your school community characterize your assets?

(13) What new skills do you believe you need to acquire for the leadership in the new millennium?
(14) How are you enhancing your knowledge and implementation of best practices?
(15) *As* a principal, what role do you play in school change and reform?
(16) What would you distinguish as top priority in your role as principal?
(17) What role do critical friends play in your role as principal?
(18) What systems do you have in place to acquire knowledge?
(19) What are the factors that have contributed to your growth and development?
(20) What do you need to realize your vision for your school?
(21) How do you seek support for development as a principal?
(22) What are your future plans for enhancing your leadership and your role as a principal?

APPENDIX F

INTERSTATE SCHOOL LEADERS LICENSURE CONSORTIMN (ISLLC STANDARDS)

Standard 1 How can you demonstrate that the success of a secondary school principal is reflected in how that leader promotes the success of all students by facilitating the development, articulation, implementation, and stewardship of a vision of learning that is shared and supported by the school community?

Standard 2 What can a secondary school principal do to promote the success of all students by advocating, nurturing, and sustaining a school culture and instructional program conducive to student learning and staff development and thereby being successful himself or herself?

Standard 3 Why would you a agree with the statement that a successful secondary school principal is the leader who promotes the success of all students by ensuring management of the organization, operations, and resources for a safe, efficient, and effective learning environment?

Standard 4 How would you show that the successful secondary school principal is the individual who promotes the success of all students by collaborating with families and community members, responding to diverse community interests and needs, and mobilizing community resources?

Standard 5 To what extent would you say that a successful secondary school principal is the educational leader who promotes the success of all students by acting with integrity, fairness, and in an ethical manner?

Standard 6 Would you say that a successful secondary school principal is the school leader who promotes the success of all students by understanding, responding to, and influencing the larger political, social, economic, legal, and cultural context?

www.ingramcontent.com/pod-product-compliance
Ingram Content Group UK Ltd.
Pitfield, Milton Keynes, MK11 3LW, UK
UKHW022227230426
12048UKWH00016BA/1101

9 781643 673806